New Things
Come into the World

New Things
Come into the World

Poems and verse-logues
of
Peter Kane Dufault

Lindisfarne Press

Some of the poems herein
have appeared in the *New Yorker,*
Atlantic, Encounter, Spectator,
and other magazines and anthologies.

ISBN 0-940262-62-2

Published by
Lindisfarne Press
RR 4, Box 94 A-1,
Hudson, New York 12534

Manufactured in the United States of America

Contents

For
Tadea, Scott, Mark, and Ethan

Early Poems

Logos

In the omniloquent harangue
of wind on a high coast
nothing else is audible.
Osprey and herring gull
on the great Apostrophe hang
mute in one place, almost

not beating their wings. Seas
explode soundlessly among
dumb caverns, and sheep,
herded by fog up the steep
headlands, move with no noise
either of hoof or tongue.

Over these, over huge sherds —
bones of a continent,
jumbled beneath the cliff —
the wind thunders, as if
now were the Beginning, it the Word,
and the Deep just now rent.

Oriole's House

Between the oriole's house
and infinity
nothing intervenes.
Literally,
it hangs among the stars;

the arc of an elm bough
is its vast orbit;
the wind lifts it from
Perseus' Helmet
to the dim nebulae

beyond Orion. Each night's
voyage of light-years
stretches far out
its twig-snap-tenure,
its teetering at

doom's delicate edge.
Thus orioles dwell
also at World's End:
Separate but equal,
their astronomical mortgage.

Fall

Whatever the maples meant —
autumnal semaphore,
yearly more violent,
in red-gold — they forebore
any plain testament.

Now they are gone, and new
houses arise instead.
These do not change their hue
nor cast acres of dead
stars to go shuffling through —

those asterisks about
some coming codicil
henceforward left in doubt:
Progress probates the will —
and Autumn is left out.

Sequitur

I follow the swallow's flight,
still, in the summer afternoon.
Because I have not caught, quite,
though twenty years are up soon,

something these seemed to promise
in blue blithe hierogram —
image or auspice
the future would redeem. . . .

Twenty whole summers now
as one netting the wind,
and nothing a man can do
in a swallow's image. Mind,

pivoting on a chance
syllable, may return
through more circumference
than loops above a barn,

turning from thought to thought,
from age to age — yet
have but been wind-caught
and tossed to a wild bet.

Swallows can fly, that's that.
Nevermind the point of view.
Crack the indeliberable gnat
of life while the sky's blue,

chuckle over it in the rain . . .
While we scuff iron shoon
through pavilions of Charlemagne
or hangars on the moon.

Half-Moon

I admire the half-moon
when — remote Jungfrau,
slopes lost in shadow
of blue afternoon —
the white rim starts to shine:

There is our highest hill,
summit to tantalize
eagle and edelweiss,
so high it couldn't still
be socketed, so fell

into the stars. Whereat
we mountaineers are called
lunatic, moon-galled,
whose cloudy ropes got caught
upon the crown of it.

Ash Can

How beautiful is the ugliness of the city
on certain days
when a heat-wave breaks and a west wind
leans on the tenement cornices,
loosening pigeons
into small tornadoes of wings;

when acres of refuse under the starved ailanthus-
trees in back alleys —
peels, bottles, cans, burnt-out pails —
sparkle; and, creaking their pulleys,
the sheets on clotheslines
thud like square-rigger sails.

Each angular canyon of laundry then is a clipper.
Its pavement heaves
like a deck and momentarily spears,
bow-geysering, legendary waves,
toward what gay occasions
from frayed posters of other years!

A Letter for All-Hallows (1949)

I am still hurt, Plin,
by your desertion. Now and again,
between rains, or among
sagged syllables on a page,
I am stopped suddenly by your grinning
lantern-jawed, monkey-eared beautiful face —
and I am hurt because you went to war
and died right in the middle of your letters
and never said goodbye.

And then your father followed you,
at a respectful distance,
and the high house on the hill went
for a Trappist monkery . . . . I hope those monks
have veneration for the juniper
and the blackberries and the frogpond
and the dust of toy-soldiers in the attic
where we warred long November afternoons.—
Above all, for the black road that,
if I listen on All-Souls' Eve, will clatter
to the gait of you riding home
from the white woods on Diamond, your horse.

The glue is long since dry
they made of him. Yet we mark well:
He was the last of the historic horses.
Revere rode him, and Sheridan,
and Sitting Bull. . . .

I hope those monks treat you gently, shades
galloping alongside the emptying meadows,
from Concord and Lexington,

from the fords of the Shenandoah,
the forks of the Little Bighorn.

Surely they would not be unmerciful
and frighten away with signs and bells and torches
so young an old-soldier and his friend
who, one way or another, were made ghosts
in all their country's wars.

Glimpse of Three Children on a Picnic

Curious how they all look alike
at this distance — about eighty yards.
Individuals resolve
into the species. There is man — his young —
eyried on blankets under an apple tree
on a steep pasture. Curious,
in this bird, the domed cranium with three dots —
two eyes, one mouth — for receiving and
transmitting signals. O beware
those three dark dots, for they have pried
into the atom's heart, predicted stars,
fathomed the sun's furnace, violated the moon.

Any clumsy beast could crush them:
delicate, pale-as-anemone shells
under the apple tree, listening
to their own private thunders — the imprisoned Sea;
the labors of mountains; tread of Tyrannosaurus,
of the Mastodon, the ages and races of Men . . .

Any clumsy beast — but none is left. O
beware those three triangulating dots, you
behemoths, tigers, wolves, hiding
in your constricting jungles. Are no claws
keen as that intellectual ordnance. It
will herd you coolly onto sharpened stakes
in a pitfall, truss you with hidden nets,
flick bullets through your heart.

Now they are looking this way — three
children of Man. What will they do?
Devour these fields? Reach up and pluck the moon?
Burn me to a cinder in dimensionless cyclotrons
of their minds? Or sing me a little song
of Gypsies and Spring?

It is very difficult to predict.
Anthropologists write about Man;
but as often Man will turn unaccountably and write
about Anthropologists, making it moot
who is classifying whom.

It is unsettling, but
in each skull
crackles a Universe.

Piper

There goes the Piper. Call him Pan.
Fingering a cylinder of wind,
he makes the sounds he only can,
till all the beasts, after their kind —

and notably the wolf and bear,
lion and lynx and fisher-cat —
dance, with their forefeet in the air
and burning moonstone eyes half shut;

dance slowly round him in a ring
with comic tails and heads a-nod.
Poor brutes, they even try to sing. . . .
O exquisite fingers on the wood,

take care, don't loosen — lest they hear,
upon the breath within, the true,
the scrannel undercry of fear.
For they'll turn then, and murder you.

On Balance

Letter to the Cape

*"We have tried to shape psychoanalysis into a general theory
of . . . human history. In this effort, the concept of sublimation
is crucial . . . and . . . there is a special connection between
sublimation and anality"* — Norman O. Brown

How is it with you, Aunt Harle,
in Wareham where the herring gulls
rake in over roofs, or reefs, of stores,
with their long grey sea-wings and sea-
voices and whitecap hulls? Of course,
I could phone down, or fly; but ei-
ther immediately annuls
a pleasant immensity —
the years and the hundreds of miles
between me and my thoughts — or between
one thought and another: That I,
far away to the west, should smell the sea —
cold, salt, clamflat, gasoline. . . .

What is it, here among hills — the keen
air, maybe, and the flying brook
begetting their annual Ishmael?
But no. I think it may be a book
I read lately, an odd
volume on history -and-psychoanal-. . .
But leave the word there, on as good
a break for sense as for typography. . . .

A book to make Man hang his head
and elevate his anus. I —
(from the other end of the genus, I
hope) — am shoresick, thinking of you
and the sea's shine in your windows,

the nearness of that *Thalassa,*
its race in your blue glance
and white smile. . . . Wordsworth's child
is with us as well as Freud's — the top
and bottom of us, right?
What would the good doctor your husband —
whose thoughts, may we say, were bottomless —
have made of it, — this "special connection
between sublimation and anality"?

                                        Hello
and ahoy anyway, Aunt Harle
to whose white clapboard, panes a-blur
with light off water, the old log
blew open again just now.
(And beyond it the herring-   and laughing-gulls,
a crescent of a white sloop heeling
under its summer sailors . . .) I'm glad
you are there, glad of the distance. It's
a damned small diameter
they'd pucker us into otherwise,
these proctologists of the soul.

'63 – '73

Unhappy country, what
wings you have, what eyes
of jellied fire, what claws
for cratering farmlands and the straw
slums of the East. Your enemies
are burning and their harvests rot;

your friends are burning and
their harvests rot. Your screams
across the world's airwaves
of Peace Peace mock their rubble graves.
Unhappy eagle, crest that gleams
among the stars, and chicken mind —

when feathers of steel moult
and over the dead paddy
dead silence supervenes,
O weep, for the world-darkening means,
the ridiculous reasons, and the bloody
and shabby pathos of the result.

American Solstice

The black brook water's win-
try **omerta,**
  its tongue of stone
and lip of ice
propound the law
now, in our solstice.

Nothing responds out there,
the needling snow's
each crystalline ar-
ticle at once
lost in the slow
spiraling silence.

An east wind wastes its breath.
The truth's too dark,
guarded, like death
in Dallas or
Danaang. . . . O mark
down a dark hour

in the black brook water's win-
try **omerta.**
  Its tongue of stone
and lip of ice
propound the law
now, in our solstice.

Letter to a Yogi

I imagine you peering out
through the showpane at Doc Platt's drugstore
at rain on the Post Road — plumes
of spray behind every tire, wipers
admonishing each other
from indignant windshields — a day
to be indoors of, and so
easing the curse of chrome,
formica and fluorescence. They
are dry anyhow; some human
comfort in that. And quieter
also, the quick-lunch crowd —
realtors, the red-haired
lady from the boutique,
the decorator with his blue poodle,
the insurance man and the lawyers —
back in their rain-caves, and no
swarm of junior-high kids heisting
candy and comic books half
the afternoon for the price of a coke.
They've been rained out.

A day to go back, in some corner
among the condoms and pills and pestles,
to your History and Heidigger.
Do you read them still?
Have you found anything?

Do you remember anything? —
Like fighting whoever passed May Bell's house,
regardless of size, because May
was your girl (though she never knew it);
and how we tangled there once and rolled
in the street till umbrella'd apart
by an elderly pacifist?

Or how, though you'd never owned skates,
and had to be towed to the cage,
you caught every puck drilled at you
and held runty Rye Neck High
two years at the top of the league?

And your buddies — Poopie and Bronzo —
the three of you yokking it up —
in the shop and the locker room . . .
Little dark violent guys,
lonely guys mostly,
short on the cars and the clothes
and the girls, clowning them out . . .

Is it lonely now, sitting there
at the vinyl and tranquilized
stimulated shampooed bubble-bathed lubricated
vibrated vaporized vitaminized
deodorized medicated mentholated
cream-pie-and-coke- and porn-fed
heart of ("what-this-place-needs-
is-a-clean-bomb") America, rain
beating on the show window?

"Yogi" we called you — after
the ballplayer, not the saint.
But maybe you'd have an answer
by now, if you're Yogi yet —
and there *are* any, past what is
is, and what aint aint.

Wishes

If we could see our own
wishes or those of another,
they would look like longspurs
or horned larks, I suppose, those brown
little birds that in cold weather
scatter, faint crucifers,

out of a cornfield or bog-hollow
blank from snow-fall — a quick
surrection of wings. They go
where we can't follow;
or come, but bring nothing back
save more cold or more snow.

Late Spring, Late Moon

The earlier dandelions lose
their lustre now, and the shadblow theirs,
and the violets theirs. But the moon's bright —
flat on one side, round on the other
like a stone lifted out of a brook — and in fact

is a stone   and is lifted
and hangs there. . . . You would think
we'd gravity enough and to spare
in one street, or one room,
or one head, to haul it hard home,
that stone kite. What wind
blows there that the weight of the world
barely can balance, barely can keep
from tearing a trillion tons of dead metal
away to leeward like a loose page
of the day's news or a wilted petal?

Winter Birches

What is it in the white birch? How
are we to construe such whiteness
as, of a dull day, over snow,
the birches are ermined in,
doing something odd to the light
so they seem to have filtered it,
or themselves are its residue: Light
without motion. . . . How

do they come to stand there
among the meltwater-blackened
maple   and hickory trunks,

coming up out of the same glum
sod — these arboreal angels you'd
think could grow only
on the summit of a white cloud?

Evensong

Last night when the sun went down
and the light lifted up — it was levered
off the last high land westward
through tier after tier of cirrus
and cumulus cloud,
all the way to the zenith — such
a *finale* of auroral cold fire
no one could speak here. We stood
like pillars of salt looking after it
a long while till it all faded
into grey and dark-grey. Oh,
how do we survive it, how
do we survive, when more than we dared dream of
is given, for no reason, and for no reason
taken away.

Valedictory Bouquet

The matter is ended now
and I have nothing to show
or keep but that once I watched her
standing beside a brook among a thousand
daffodils with her head tipped — so —
like theirs;   and I thought just now
I saw her familiar white
smock far away in a field, but
it was only the white shadblow.

Blackbirds

Well, the blackbirds came back. . . .
We knew they would. Still —
seven months at a crack —
and winds can blow ill.

We've known those in less
interval could forget
name, number, address. . . .
How sad to admit

there was mockery almost
in the *Fragmites* grass
with a blackbird aboast
on every blade, as,

tails tucked underneath,
they teetered and chirred,
simply keeping the faith
without knowing the word.

Vignette of a Lake in Winter

The astonishing eloquence of it —
all those square miles of water
come-on abruptly, at sundown,
where the road rounds a high contour . . . Flat
as a palette and flaming —
the whole westward arc of it —
with a cold plum color, the east
coves covered in white ice,
and the center black, black as a polar
solstice. I wasn't set
for this sudden vast remission
in the ups and downs of the world. How
could one not succumb
to such level insistence, not
stop cold and consider
the solitary grebe there, its wake,
from a point utterly random
on the flamboyant face of the deep,
widening to include more, more,
and finally all, of the universe?

Reunion at a Summer Place

Dear, it is the stars' imperium
that makes us paupers, all
that glittering multitude
turning till Kingdom Come
in their grand gradual
galliard, robed in eternity.
What have we
but a few rags — a day, a night
thrown down — of all that dazzle and darkness;
a Summer, a Fall,

a motley of seasons. . . . Dressed
so, we may play the fool
for a Time that meanwhile grinds
our faces in the dust. . . .
Oh you'd stay virginal
and fugitive as the Pleiades
if things were otherwise,
and I'd be taller than Orion. But —
we are born too far from favor,
from where identical

August comes on — candescent night
millraced with foam-white stars,
those tireless dancers
shod in meteorite.
Our twenty ridiculous years
pass while the same instant
of eternity's on the Firmament,
the light's in mid-leap from Arcturus. . . . Look,
old clown, a joke for Coma Berenice
are these greyed hairs of ours.

On a Painting of a Mastodon in a Child's Picture Book

The Mastodon's gone
whose eight-ton tread
shook the steppes of the earth;
above whose head
wheeled condors wide as storms,
their necks blood-red.

With them, he is gone
out the gates of ice
and quagmire, to his cold
bed, to fossilize.
In all eternity, none
will now lay eyes

upon his mountainous
haired hump, describe
his mating thunders, his
stance toward the tribe
of men; no priest of Pan
ever imbibe

the groping divinity
that heaved that hulk,
heavy with ivory, forward
out of the black
cone forest and grey muskeg,
snows on his back.

He might have known
something of the power-
and-the-glory, whose withers rose

like the shore
of an iceberg, and whose bones
a billionth year

barely will break. . . .
   But, long since, he's
utterly felled . . . . Sometimes it makes
the imagination freeze,
my dears, how unsentimental
God really is.

Perspective

Sarder's farm fades
into scenery at half a mile; a cer-
tain quantity of tin cans
and dead bedding that defilades
down into the brook mer-
cifully blotted at this distance;

and it, abstract — a sleep-
ing castle with silo towers —
flat, monumental as
some weathering Norman keep
a hundred years of hours
broke on like arrows of glass

and couldn't change. (Sarder's
not moved to the Town yet
nor the Town spread to him.)
Likewise geographers,
reading our green planet
from Mars or the moon's rim,

must make our holocaust-
ic continents mere blurs
of their bombed selves: silent
gryphons, sphinxes embossed
on the immovable waters. . . .
Philosophy also — bent

on generalities:
They're all that saves the world
from its details — its sunk
sheds, rotting Chevrolets,
its Beatle bathos hurled
at stripped fields bright with junk.

Fisherman

I have been fishing now
for nine hours, and in that time
departed all cortical things,
having turned gradually below-
light to dim strata of slime-
weed, bass and shoaled fingerlings.

Plover-like, peering offshore,
where nothing is certain, save
the infrequent rational gleam
of the lure, like a drowned flare,
on its long retrieve
signalling into the unseen.

For hours, for half a day
nothing may answer. Then —
double double tug: some cold
killer of fry, fathoms away,
reasserts a Silurian
mindless violence. Hauled

in, he will thrash, expressionless,
body one clenched limb for
sword-cuts in the deep. Sun-
fish, maybe, with daggered crest
like Neptune's helmet, gold gor-
get and turquoise menton.

Or pickerel, the miniature
barracuda, whose fine scale
is like mica or gold leaf. Some-
times I feel like a doctor
of dreams — like Jung or a sybil —
identifying, as they come

frantic into daylight, this
or that gaudy and innocent
archaism. But each pulls
the angler lakeward also, as
it sounds against the bent
spinrod and dragged reel.

I would not dare go down
into that inverted world where
symbols devour other symbols
in darkness. No, it was on-
ly this morning I woke from there —
God knows upon what impulse.

Hills

The simple seriousness of hills —
dull humps and withers, brown
with stubble or moss-green,
bent as if they could graze,
or maybe were praying — old fidels,
foreheads against the hidden stone —
foreheads and knees . . .

Their simple gravity is so great
that they can pull a man down too
to *his* knees, if he look suddenly
at them; as if the will
crumbled, confronted with such weight
as hauls their long slopes downward through
field after field and holds them still

a thousand thousand years. Sometimes,
passing them in a car, cornered,
clock-ridden, you can almost weep
for wanting to walk out or run
the length of their dry-cymes,
dead-leaves, blackbird-
empty aphelion

till Spring — or Ice, or Inland Sea —
come round again, and lose this hour-
hand hewing at our lives. Oh, hills
have time and time and time
to try the dust's humility,
and strengthen prophets and empower
lovers by their long paradigm.

Snow

Number itself goes numb under
its simple addition, zeroes and nines
make but a poor retort
to its fury of finities. If
even for a single instant,
between here and the dark
tepees of the woods yonder, God
had to count the snowflakes,
it would never snow.

Trillions, quadrillions are a cup
soon filled between a house and barn.
Not all the falcon-plundered
swans of the world could so down
that white tornado-ing corridor.
Something else — meteorologies —
clouds and cold air —
meet, mindlessly formulate,
and suddenly everywhere
over a hundred, a thousand square
miles, precipitate, without reckoning what
casual enormities the geo-
metrical townships are buried under.

One Gothic individual crystal
gets caught on the long mane
of our neighbor's mare,
and a vast theological problem,
a band of angels, pivots
upon an asterisk: It turns
in a trice to mist or melt.
But what formal intensity ar-
ticulated it out of nothing

a moment ago? Nobody understands
the mind of a crystal;
or the tie of art to mere elements,
or of self to the rags and cinders
of its long nonentity.

Ruth

She lies now in the long
dawn in a room mid-maple high.
She sleeps. Twenty million leaves
clatter, conveying the blue-green-gold
light to the south and east windows
minted into their millionfold
swivelling shadows. Under the eaves
jays bluster, ravening among
numbed wasps, too slow either to sting or fly.

She'll wake up soon and go down
to the Labrador pup slobbering with joy,
seven cats with their tails in the air,
six diffident hens by the back door,
old gelding grumbling at his rail fence —
as contented to feed them as to sleep some more.
She is content either here or there,
the way clouds are: Sort of a con-
densation of kindness with no alloy.

Clouds and sun too. She brings
gardens out of the bare ground

outdoors or in. On the south side
of the house not a window sill
but is jungled with marjoram,
lemon verbena, saffron, dill.
She pities them, pinches their dried
leaves off — and either talks or sings
something they understand

and answer in all their flowers. Her
age is a half mine, but I think
is also ancient, like the race
of women itself. I could not tell —
but she could — the way Esther, bring-
ing nothing but her own softness, mel-
ted an iron king; or with what grace
Rebekah, further back, in Ur,
made Abraham's tired camels drink.

Centenarian

Senility gives greater pause
than death does: Auntie Brooke
now babbles and knows no one.
Though we all mind what she was —
the beloved matriarch
and inveterate clown.

And had death intervened, even
at ninety, wouldn't we all
agree she'd still taken (as
the phrase is) to heaven
a light   wry and jovial
as ever it was?

But for *this*, for *this*, we've scant
theology: the slow
living-entropy of the mind.
Not merely indifferent,
she tries to know,
and is not deaf or blind

but as though drowning — the soul
drowning in the body, even
as that's drowning in time.
Till we ask if a Black Hole
must govern here, not a heaven,
let alone reason or rime.

Notes on a Woodcock

I searched for a woodcock I'd heard
twittering in the bluegrey caverns
of evening — a sardonic bird
with the long droll proboscis
of the born belittler — in his case
so long it belittles himself.
About starling size
he is — with like wedge-shaped wings
and tail, so that he too flutters
a faint four-pointed star
overhead where he hovers and sings
down to his maybe-more-amused-
than-moved beloved in the grass.
Anyway, at concert's end
he descends in a teetering spiral
like a drunk coming down from a box
at the opera — and after a brief silence
utters a loud piercing razzberry,
five or six times.

But, passion or parody,
his twitter among the ragged last
white clouds blown eastward
and nightward is like an English lark's,
and you'd look up too, hearing it,
to try to make him out . . . I did,
and picked up a small star all right —
so — for that demi-flash before
it registered as Vega early alight —
saw clearly a golden woodcock.
And then the very illusion's fading
made Vega seem to recede
singing into infinity. Oh,

he took me in, that parodist,
and lost me where no berries grow.

Anthill In Winter

I knocked with my hard heel
on their hard roof
but got no answer — black
panic, nor red reproof.
I could almost feel,

like Roland at his Dark
Tower, the knock go down
through vaults and galleries
where all had turned to stone;
and where a distant arch-

eological tap-tap
would no more be heard
than in Herculaneum
the hammers of Charles Third
upon ages of pumiced sleep.

What trumpet will sound when
that brittle, basalt-hewn
queen and her catafalques —
sure as the crack of June —
melt into mortals again?

At That Hour

At that hour over snow
when there are both day- and moon-
light and the trees cast two shadows

I think of you —
how you were of two minds. . . .
        I would like to show,

standing beside you,
how the red light and the blue light
are crossing among the con-

volutions of an elm —
that is like the pen-sketch of a brain,
with its regions and lobes,

its Fissure of Orlando —
crossing, unreconciled,
and each tracing on snow

its opposite version (How
clearly they lie, one east,
one west);   and tell you:

Nevermind, my dear. We too
cast complementarities. All
our lies likewise were true.

Wild Geese Going Over

The awesomest flock of wild geese I ever saw
passed over just after sundown.
Three hundred or more, their arrows
and echelons, their mile-wide
order-of-advance wavering
as though under fire, their bagpipes—
chanters and drones — blowing,

their battle dress flashing —
each grey cuirass — where at three-thousand
feet they still had bright daylight
and caught it — a multiple lens
shuttered by wingbeats, twinkling
like hundreds of running-lights.

They passed over so far up,
so musical, indistinct, shimmering,
we'd have known — once — we stood under
an exaltation of angels.
(There was even one *black* one — a satan? — haunting
that shining host, alone not shining,
absorbing the light . . .) As it was,
our neighbor, Bernie, said only,
"Those fuckers are really *up* there!" —

Which is O.K. He'd have said that for angels.

Leaving a Station — Sunday, February 1, 197*

You're on the train
and gone now. . . . Driving home,
I hear the diesel horn from Martindale,
and again, faintly, from Craryville.
A dying sound . . .

A dying beast,
bellowing its last into the frozen swamps;
struck and sold short and kept moving
by court order and the trainman's curse . . .

                          Young man,

you aren't riding in style,
nor on any wave
save the dead ebb of one
Cornelius Vanderbilt strode, glittering
onto a remote reef of the Century.

Even so, it pulls us apart —
eleven miles long and lengthening,
our last handgrip across the grinding wheels. . . .
I hadn't finished. What was it
I meant to tell you?

            Someone, when I was four,
            pointed out overhead an eagle. It shed rings
            of vertigo and of glory.
            And again, at eighteen, a first snow
            falling among oak leaves and swamp candles—
            a molt of time — rustled
            around me like Ecclesiastes — *gentle*
            erasure and a cold elation.

Beside me the heavy slab
of the TIMES lies like a tombstone
scored with the epitaphs of the World. The Whole
System is Breaking Down. Money has moved
on, out of rails, into madness
and real estate on the moon,
futures in black air and dead waters,
a corner on cobalt, a bull
market in Terra-cide. No   no,

I should have asked forgiveness —
because I could not save the last eagle
and already the golden bowl is broken
and the pitcher is broken at the cistern. . . .

Whatever it was I hollered
finally, a last hedge
on such an investment of life's blood
into a dying railroad —
those old bone-jarring trucks and couplings
shrieking toward Desperate City — I've tears now
for trains the fathers have taken
that set the sons' teeth on edge.

Farm Animals at Evening

How benignly the night
deepens above dumb beasts, those slow
bodies bowed in their disappearing fields
to the roots of humility. They
nevermind the dark, and them eternity
touches but lightly on the back
with its streamers and grand emerging
geometries of the Zodiac.
To them, for whom there is no time like ours,
only the dumb immediate instant — no
legends and no astronomies — the sun
is already out of mind
forever — and the Universe
a steep dunged moor, tasselled
with silver trefoil and the white moonshine.

Preview

If it were to be
like setting a saw down,
tired, while your glance mounts
casually through a black diagram
of midwinter maples to the moon's
Euclidian purity, to the orbits of the stars . . .

Dying, that is, body
old saw, placed on its horse
or hearse, from weariness,
while — cold, illumined — one immense
Mathematic takes its place — radix
beneath our sawdust days, in its branches the
      light-years . . .

Love's Actuarity

No wonder they made him blind —
Cupid — and gave him arrows.
In two strokes, so, they defined
the odds of love and the sorrows.

The energy of desire
confronts the Probable —
so random, though, in its fire
a queen may well love a bull,

or an old man a child.
A barb is no less a curse
that the archer shot it wild.
You can't yank in reverse

without doubling the cut,
nor push through as it's sent —
for less than your life — what
arrived by accident.

Katydids

In the night   all night
every three feet   from window
to world's end   their myriads
morselessly tap
tap tap   the call letters
S(. . .)   I(. .)   H(. . . .)
to a world they don't dream of.

Come in S . . . Come in H . . . .

But they are busy with time
and don't hear us. Because
they have but a summer — no,
less than a summer, the gold-
enrod and bittersweet
end of a summer is all; and time
itself's their nectar.   Tap

tap tap   the invisible kegs
of second after second, frothed
with Aquila, Cygnus, the Crown . . . High
in the tremendous taverns of the trees,
they are not aware of us,
the mere dregs.

Propriety

When asked what I thought of her
I said she seems very nice.
Not, though, that I'd been surprised
into a kind of erotic dislike,
an impulse to rape, to taste
in full that austere excise
of everything but the brisk,
buckled, perfunctory, chaste;
feel it unclew,
shudder and go, leaving naught
but wilderness — yes — un-nice
naked necessity. . . .
I am properly ashamed of the thought
and would tell no one but you.

Vera Frost — (1904–1972)

What to do with our dead . . . We beg
pardon, good neighbor; no offense is meant
if your old broken body (turned
briefly to marble) now we drag
through all we have ever thought on death. . . .

Shy as an ovenbird, sometimes
she would hide from her friends, and surely
it is nothing of hers, this immense
centrality. Surely among all the voices
and phone calls and importance of cars coming
and going up the dirt road
there is shrilly absent her own
exasperated   "Oh
for god's sake, take it out and bury it!"

. . . Which ceased like an old horse folding
its knees in a field, or a gull
offshore and alone, the sea
(or the hills)
seconding with a wave
that is neither hail nor farewell. Indeed,

it is more like looking seaward
into simple geometry
or at hills above timberline
than "seeing-for-the-last-time"
someone we knew. Who'd have believed
she could be so indifferent, either
to our love or our nuisance,
as to lie still and say no more,
nor less, than the face of a cliff?

59

Yet she always meant what she said,
and vice versa. This, then, must be it:
an indifference so great
(and all the greater if
in cold contrast to a bent
beloved figure and funny hat)
it frightens us, being what no one
can compass and live.

Of course, we do not yet know
what "live" means. —
To have been timid,
yet stubborn?
To have known no man,
to have kept Shetland ponies and cats,
to have sagged into old age, toil-
broken at fifty-five?

To have held together an in-
computable cosmos of cells?
To have come and gone like a frost-
crystal, by sidereal time?

One morning she hauled a dead fowl
to the fox-den up on the kame. She knew
who it was fled with a swish and a thud
at midnight, dumping his ballast.
She figured he'd earned it — and "the damn hen
was dead anyhow" . . . One time,
she was paid-down on a house
in the next state, her goods half packed;
and had so much fun at the farewell party
she was still here ten years later. —
Still doing the cooking, the barn chores (a ton
of dung every day), the garden,
the Shetland breeding and showing — but more
slowly each year, the flesh

heavier on the bone, the bone
bleaker with damp when the wind
swung easterly. You could say:
"The poor soul wore herself out", or:
"She had not been happy of late."

But who is? — and don't
we pursue rather than have
happiness? Almost by definition,
then, it is somewheres else —
a moving target we have to lead a little
to wing at all. . . .

From the vantage point of a pile
of packing crates, all but moved,
she could see suddenly, and behind her,
the elusive aura.
Quiet now, she may know
whether it's better to be worn out
by dragging your own rainbow
or by running after it, dragging
everything else.

And what to do with the dead
when we are not allowed
to bury them under the Ben Davis trees
in the orchard, or heap up old pony traps,
saddles and studbooks and ribbons,
and sprinkle with gasoline and let it all go
and the dead with it straight up
into the sky . . . One thing,
at least, needn't worry us:
If there's little talk about God
and Hereafter and angels (which she
would have none of) What *is* —
and what *was*, Vera — surely
are catechism enough.

Three Old Ponies

They're gone now, with all they know:
how to be haltered, led,
and bullied into a van. . . .

It doesn't seem much to bring
to a total reckoning. But
no more questions are asked
at that horse show. They'll step
humbly under their headstalls
from the truck-gate, one by one,
into a .22 bullet point-
blank at "an imaginary X
between the eyes and ears" . . . So much
for a-little-knowledge-as-a-dangerous-thing.

For the rest of it, their dumb drift
of stars/rain/flies/snow/
wind blowing down out of the hemlocks —
never touching the one thing they knew —

must have been like our dreams —
of a vast provenience, yet
ambiguous as to time or place,
logic or meaning. . . . Almost
one can imagine it goes on for them,
that dream: forty acres of poor
pasture — come fall   come winter   spring   summer —

and little changed, only
by twelve hooves quieter than it was
and the wild strawberries
less trodden on.

The Mud Dauber Wasp

I take heart, breaking in
to the drab little pueblo
of a dauber wasp: Inside,
wrinkled as a raisin
and rigid as Pharoah
embalmed and mummified,

the dauber's pupa-doll
sits in its shroud or pod —
a mere seed of a thing,
a bean, cold as the wall
it crooked against, and god-
forsaken now, though Spring

comes in a week . . . And god-
forsaken anyway,
for all entomologies —
or maths, or rockets — could
coerce its crumb of clay
to a metamorphosis.

And yet — the first warm days
suffice. A shudder in
the faint magnetic field? —
and undifferentiate clay's
quick, visual, wearing thin
wings — and at last unsealed

it flies away. No wonder
Pharoah lay spiralled in
a caul of similar kind
when he went under ground. Or
that I take heart — who've been
bowed-down, and barren of mind.

End View of a Cedar Log

Before I burn
any of this cedar,
I will have to marvel
a while at its wine-red
marrow, like a bright ore

in the bones of a mountain, buried;
a color yet not a color
in the absolute introverse
where it formed, locked from any light.

Here it turns up by accident —
and axe, a branch having snapped
from snow — this unsettling mandala
with its lustre of satin and porphyry —
never meant to be seen at all. . . .
Yet meant for something. — Something

unsuperficial, like grace
perhaps, or however we see in a dark
room in a dark skull the purples and ivories
of our improbable dreams.

A Shell

And here's this shell of a crab,
this implosive symmetry   worn
by a long storm of cis-marine light
to a thing white as sea-salt and weightless
as a wasp nest. Two lobes
only — the claws gone
out of their portholes — two
matching lobes left, (and right)
like a brain's . . . It's amazing

at what minute tolerances something,
though crushed under the sea's grey
palisades of shuddering iron,
details this ineffable cortex — not
to mention others, ashore —
by the billions, and in utter indifference,
or as if dissatisfied, casts
every last one away.

In an Old Graveyard

One is struck by the *form*,
or *closure* to these lives — the stone
chord of their repose   that presses
up into the wind forever
certain keys of greyed granite.

The Crowne family: Fourteen
graves in a ring, untended
yet legible still. They seem
to have taken it well — in strict
order, you might say — disaster. It couldn't break
the family circle nor erase the name.

Of course they ordained it — some
such bright morning maybe as this
with the young hawks coasting and calling
in the white foam of the clouds,
in the time of the wild blackberries. . . .

INFANT CHILD   INFANT CHILD
MOTHER   NETTIE   SILAS   HAROLD

how and where they would form themselves
for that last cold Public Appearance —
in which we encounter them these
hundred years later — we
who are here   or are not here more
like smoke   or like frost,   everything
with us is so open-ended.

Lines from Wales

I wait for the herring gull
to fall off in the wind
thudding all day on the bluffs
where the road drops from Pennralltygardde
through sheep-sorrel down to the sea.

Surely wings are the wrong thing
for standing in one place.
This day, the downturn of a feather
could scale him to Cardigan,
twenty miles on the Pembrokeshire Coast.

Even the cows move. I wonder
and wonder how a herring gull
without mathematics resolves
on a point in space — the space
rushing under him, too, like time —

and hangs there, perfectly still,
an equation of grey wings. —
While I've blown away like thistle
three thousand miles to Glanrhyd
and left all I love behind.

Great Grandmother

She is going, we think.
Old and translucent and tiny
and light as the wreck of a sparrow
or a wasp on a sill, she seems
to have passed through now
an invisible wall of pain

and begins already
to see us with the utter detachment
of one looking into a bowl
where a few colored fish hover
in a volume of pure caprice.

'Cool'

Cool, in the long barn
the wind blows through and the blue-
enamelled and saffron swallow —
barb out of a   bow-in-the-clouds —
whips to his clay vase
full of fierce little faces . . .

I pretend he is not there — or
that I am not here — an effacement,
considering here's naught else then
but dung, perhaps too profound
by a fork's length. But if
I look straight at him, he'll fly.

I wish him no harm. I'd be happy
if once he'd alight on my hand
and I held it all here an instant —
that wind-world he can turn,
with a tilt of a feather, softer
than pollen or taut as ice —
to skate on those blue blades
in the fjords of the summer cumulus.

But haven't I learned by now
the hunter's, soldier's, lover's guile
or 'cool' — how not to be there,
how the heart's-desire takes,
or is taken, unaware?

The Quality of Mercy

That much is clear at least: A man
owes nothing to tent-caterpillars
and is free to put their damned gobs
of snot-colored gauze to the torch,
with fried worms falling out of the trees
like shit through a sieve. . . . But here —
though we'll not be thanked for it — even

here, we're in sight of the line
between what we can and can't do;
and, finding the scorched survivors
writhing in the grass, trample
them mercifully into green glue.

A First Night

It's the first night, I suppose,
in more than eighty year
Hattie has slept alone. . . .
And outdoors, in the falling
snow, without bedclothes
or night light and none near
but the deaf sunken stone
were one to awaken calling.

What could old Hattie have done
wrong, anyway? — Made raw-
milk cheese, rubbed eggs, admired
her rose-red Christmas cactus, and
rocked, looking out at one
more mid-February thaw,
drifts melting and dungwagon mired —
that now like a reprimand

she might have heard sixty-eight
or seventy years ago,
(such as 'Hattie thinks she is clever,
but will go to bed with boxed ears
and no supper') she is told: 'Tonight
you'll sleep with shoes on in the snow
in the cemetery and never
never wake up in a million years.'

Hemlocks — April, '80

They stand, each half a bole higher
up the bare hornstone — old bone
of the world broken
before the Miocene — their green
caverns ravening wind, sun,
white cloud and bright air,
cries of the hylas. Higher
than houses they are, and higher
still for the hill under them
and full of gold glints and old
winter gloom in their crowdark steeples.

And can they, for all their fathoms-
and-fathoms-deep converse with the light,
be blind — and, for all their whistling
and trestling, deaf — neither seeing not hearing
themselves nor the matted monks'-cloth
acres tumbling buff-colored into the greenblush
of April   and the frogs' comic
and cacophonous chorus, "Rack-
ety-ax-ax, rackety- . . ." Ex-
actly!   Exactly how
to be beautiful: to know
nothing, nothing of it at all,
to be still waving in Eden
a million Aprils ago.

A Psychological Weapon

I ventured it with the Old Gentleman once
not many Thanksgivings ago —
'The Gettysburgh Question'. I guess
sire and son were at sword's points yet,
that, as though for the fun's sake,
I could throw fifteen thousand banshee-
lunged Confederates at him — Hood's
Division of Longstreet's Corps.

A pandemonium of ghosts,
surely . . . What was he, though,
at eighty-seven, but a gaunt and irascible
old spectre himself?   "Way back there,"
he used to tell us, "Back there
when I was a little fella
could still walk under a horse,
the Troops on Memorial Day
wore *blue*. They were Union veterans,
men who'd fought at Antietam, Cold Harbor,
The Wilderness. . . . Farmers, most of 'em.
They worked too hard to get fat
and their uniforms still fit 'em.
They made a sight, I can tell you.
They knew how to march, those fellas.
Straight up. And proud. They'd licked Lee
and they looked ready to do it again, too.
Marching wasn't just holiday stuff either,
not in their day, y'understand. Men marched
under fire, elbow to elbow, lines
dressed on the guidons and drummers behind 'em.
Drummers! They kept in step, by God!
And that's how they went in —
into musketry or a cannonade.
No other way to mass your firepower

in those days but to mass your men.
And they died. God, they died.
A thousand men down at a volley. You wonder
any ever came back.

But these did, somehow. So us kids,
even if it was forty years later,
knew what real soldiers looked like."

                                              History
had most of him, all but this
deaf, trembling, papery remnant.
Even his own war — Wilson's War —
had been all bright brass and buffed leather
and salutes taken on horseback:
Post Adjutant he was then
at Fort Monroe in Virginia —
a coastal battery, ready

but never used — a museum, really,
of the old Regular Army: parades
and punctilio, shades
of General Winfield Scott and Old Dominion days.

When my own time came, I
with my grommetless "fifty
mission crush" in the cap
and two years overseas
was never a soldier to him.

Nor ever much of anything to him, having
a mystical turn of mind.
You could say I enjoyed being puzzled. —
(What's puzzlement, really, but
a degree of wonder? And what's wonder
again but a kind of psychedelic, a glimpse
of infinite possibilities?)

Nothing of that for him.
A puzzle calls for analysis,
analysis leads to decision,
and there it ends. A practical man:
Thirty years in big corporate management.
(And we'd fought there, too: myself
Jeffersonian, ul-
timately pastoral, I suppose;
and him Hamiltonian, northern,
pro-consul of industrial empire.)

But back of that, like a patent
of ancient and chivalric nobility,
loomed those two years at field grade
in the Old Regular Army. Nor
could he have forgotten it had he tried to,
for it seemed no one else could.
He remained "The Major," from boardroom
to secretarial pool. And I recall him
still rasping into the hall phone
in his eighties, "This is the Major. . . ." So
I was calling his bluff, be-
latedly. (But what isn't
belated, in a demurral to History?) Yet
I was at once sorry I'd done it.
The cornered, outraged glare
he flashed at me silenced all tables —
four generations of us, none of whom
had come up with the answer. He was too deaf
to have heard the question till then,
and sat there, smiling at the pantomime.

I'd not grasped how little was left
of the old exec but his dignity,
and how I'd be challenging that,

taking the high ground of him
for an odd scrap of book-learning. . . . I'd
have backed out, had he not rebuked me:
   "I'd need more information than that!" he snapped.
"Decisions aren't made in a vacuum."

   I repeated the particulars:

Gettysburgh. Second day.
July 2, 1863 . . .
The Twentieth Maine Infantry,
Col. Joshua Chamberlain, C.O.,
on a hill — "Little Round Top": The regiment
has repulsed three successive attacks
from the right wing of Hood's Division.
A fourth assault is now massing
beyond the Devil's Den. The Twentieth Maine
stands unsupported, Col. Chamberlain
having been flank-marched abruptly here,
along with other elements of Skyes Fifth Corps
not yet in sight. Beyond those
in his own thinned ranks, not a blue blouse
can be seen, save far to the north
where regiment after blue regiment
stretches out along Meade's chosen line.

Rebel cannon on this hill
will enfilade the entire Army of the Potomac
and the battle be over before it starts. The odds,
even figuring those appalling windrows
of Brady corpses in the Devil's Den,
are still about five-to-one
against the Twentieth Maine.

Col. Chamberlain is now informed
his men are out of ammunition.

What does he do?

The Major frowned in silence a while,
then looked at me almost mildly.
"They attacked three times?"

   "Three times. And forming up for the fourth."
He scowled again, then suddenly struck the table.
"Fix bayonets!" he croaked; then
in a full voice roared out, "Charge!"

"Hey, Gramp," cried a grandson,
"That's the other side. What did our side do?"

"No!" he shot back.
"I don't know what that fella did . . ."
He fixed me with his dim bristly gaze,
"But that's what he shoulda done!"
                       No doubt
my open-mouthed stare told him
he'd hit the answer. He sat back
with an air of grim satisfaction.
                    "Charge?"
someone whimpered in disbelief.
                  "Certainly.
The bayonet is a psychological weapon.
Damn few fellas ever got stuck with one."

He turned to me again:
"The rebels broke, didn't they?"

I nodded.
    "Of course they did.
What they'd been through, they'd've run
'f you'd sic'd a cross dog on 'em.
That's basic infantry tactics, or it was

in my day. Still is, I wouldn't wonder.
That fella made the correct decision.
No more, no less.
Nothing miraculous in it at all. . . ."

I can't say I was not proud
of the old martinet. . . . One of the kids
ran over and pumped his hand, crowing
"Gimme five, Gramp! You saved the Union!"

The Major did not smile.

He died not long after, at ninety,
and took History with him —
save for a sensation I get
at times when I think of him
that something in me will forever
be falling back toward the Potomac.

The White Witch

"Agrimony for melancholy . . .
Borage to banish fear . . .
Fenugreek for full flesh . . .
Yarrow for wounds by iron . . .
Amanita, the death-cap . . .
Mandrake . . . They are all here,"

the White Witch notes. And again
(with a certain cogency):
"If here is the leaf of death,
hasn't life its leaf?" (She is seeking,
like a Ponce de Leon,
the sprig of immortality.)

" 'Hope is a thing . . .' Why not
pleasure, courage, belief,
love? Or are those so rare
some reverse-amanita can't
summon them from thin air
into a root or leaf?

And whether thereby we push
spirit out of the world, or push
matter out of the world,
who cares — if naught's left un-
accounted for, if it happen
God Himself is a Burning Bush?"

On Italo Svevo's "As a Man Grows Older"

I too, once, Emilio Brentani . . .
Even to the walk — the nonchalant swing
bannered with bright hair — even
to the "thin red curve of her mouth outlined
against bright teeth . . ." Why is it
the likes of her drop their sunshades
for the likes of us to retrieve? Why
do they listen, downcast,
to our love and confess their own,
and flinch as if struck if we say
"I must leave early,"   and all the while
be betraying or prepared to betray?

No answer from you, Emilio.
The best you could do was yell
"Whore!" and throw a stone after.
But I can imagine Ange
at eighty, "a smoke-dried stick",
toothless in Trieste, croaking,
with a justice that cracks my heart:

"Did he own the sea, that he swam in it?
Or the sun and moon that they shined on him?
And I was more beautiful than all of them
in my day!"

Goshawk

That harbinger of God's hardness, North
American Goshawk — storm-
grey above, ice-grey beneath — segment
of a winter azimuth — de-
tached herself from this morning and
seized a black hen   and caromed
thirty yards through the soft snow, wrenching
feathers and flesh out, too
blood-crazy to kill clean. . . .

                              Tell me
if it's not hard how a haggard
hasn't even the hangman's mercy
but tears the heart out alive — that she
should have been made so;

and so, too, that when the dog
ran yapping and drove her off,
the grey crucifer levitated
in such a cold pride of windblown
lightness over the tines of the trees

you'd have forgiven her, even
if she could have torn
in that worse way there is:
with a word, never breaking the skin.

Burden

I called you because I could not stand alone
looking north to that skyline-
tree globed with its yellow apples
balancing like a fountain of planets
in the bright light and the blue air.

And because on the way there
I looked at a smooth cirque
the brook had worn in a stone;
and nothing as soft as water
could, by taking care,
have so pestled and polished
that granite mortar; only
by a thousand years of indifference,
of aiming elsewhere.

I wish we might do — or no,
look back and find we had done —
some un-advertized thing,
overwhelming and un-self-aware
as water streamlining a stone, or a tree's
kindling in an empty meadow
its casual Hesperides.

Small Wild Creatures Along a Road at Night

Not to be seen . . . Not to be seen . . .
We can hardly conceive
such a curse on the light,
such a love of oblivion, as
in the weasel's dense muscular
bolt from the highbeam;
the fox's flattening cringe
into his shadow; the rac-
coon's shambling retreat
on the road-shoulder, his coat
humped up over his head. They mean

not to be there, or anywhere; hence
are the night's minions — and all
the more if there's no moon
and a black cloudcast, so
that by padding upwind and with care
they're extinguished in five senses. With
what an ill grace they incarnate
again in the glare like borers
wedged out of a blind heartwood
to unwelcome apocalypse; with
what relief, evidently, re-enter
such a void as our vanity,
its name written in lights,
shudders at, and accelerates.

April 14, 1981

The nine a.m. news from here is:
it was four degrees below freezing
though mid-April; and a greybeard man
ran west under a grey sky, though
he could not catch up the youth
who'd grabbed his name and fled;
and a grey horse, rump to the weather, came
head-up, tense as a deer,
to stare at him directly
out of the Stone Age; and a grey
migrating goshawk beat
into the wind overhead. . . . Indeed,

all the while Young and Crippen rode
their rocket into a well
bouldered with planets and back again,
it was all *retro* here:

in the hills' draughty museum, these
grey antiquities.

The November Meteors

They are not falling so much
as intersecting — their orbit
or spacetime with ours — the Leonids —
at a closing velocity
of forty-four miles per second. Each time
you see it — the forty-four-mile
streak of incinerating nickel and iron,
and the second, a cicatrice
high in the ionosphere
on the fixity of our assumptions.

For we thought it a still night — white
frost on the fencerail and the only leaves left,
the oaks', motionless, where we stood
stargazing, out of earshot
of politics, commerce and war. Now
we are flashed new coordinates,
with the oaks and huge humps of the hills
and the whole country and continent
hurtling toward Taurus at sixty-five thousand
miles per hour — and, abruptly, our own
cancelled seconds and minutes
like so many answering streaks
on a runaway and oblivious blackness.

Farm Houses (Off the Taconic Parkway)

Sometimes in an absolute sense
it seems they are passed — Past — these
houses presiding over a half-mile
of brown horse-road and a rail fence,
that pivot grandly behind their striding trees,
recede and are lost   while
we wheel by them at seventy, seventy-five
miles an hour, sitting perfectly still,
the body not in it at all, only the will.

It's as if we could watch them slip
into their own preterite — house and yard
bumped by some co-efficient of
cosmic expansion: Time speeded up. . . .
        I remember a certain blue, white-starred
trainer taxi-ing the rough
edge of a field in a racketing, dew-bright
cow-astounded Spring — a ship so blurred
now in the world's rocketry tomorrow-ward

the mere thought of it folds its wings
away among the lances of Arthur's knights
and its fluttering fuselage stalls beside
their high horses of parchment. Groundling
till then, I solo'd, staggering to the heights
of trees, and saw them slide
backward and down, saw towns of Tennessee
dwindle to dominoes, my shouts
drowned in the noise, the engine's iron salutes

to the glory of it, the wonder. . . . Who then
could imagine settling in, going slow,
building fence, letting sleeping dogs lie?
This sidelong look, aft and down

off the Taconic at a turning windrow,
brings it back now, and is also why
I think I would re-define Time-Past as something
those in it can't leave behind fast enough —
then find it was who they are, or what they love.

Chords

   Where we are at a given instant
with respect to others we think of
who may or may not think of us
seems to form chords at times — silent,
to our ears at least,
yet intense as music —
on a board fretted with separate cities. We
are pressed down, one here, one there,
in our patterns. I can't help
wondering *Whose* fingers we are, cut or callused
on the steel threads of our days,

and what sound goes up,
or if no sound goes
and it's all wasted, the fierce
virtuosity vaulting us
one from another, and often
at great speed. If it made
music, perhaps then
it would be more bearable. Aeons from here
the stars too are trapped
in their chord-patterns   the ancients
claimed made a music they could hear.

Brick

Does it suffer
from an excess of formality? Square
as an assertion of rectitude, it
is incorruptible, comes always
unchanged through the fire. What
could be more ideal
for administering correction — notes
Ignatz-the-Mouse   who
utilizes its irreducible gravity
on the pretensions of Krazy Kat.
(Whereat Officer Pup
hauls him off to the brickhouse.) Brick
is simply available for rebuke
and itself impartial. Still,
remembering these, I suspect
there's a metaphysical brick
with aerodynamic properties —
enough to hang in mid-chuck
for — what is it — forty years? —
since Herriman drew it there
en route from Mouse to Kat
under a stranded moon
in a mysteriously changing
landscape of mesas.   But

why a brick?
Well they say the poor fellow was stoned
most of the time, no pun
intended. The imperturbable
balance of any brick
on its long axis must be considered.

Maybe a brick just is
(to Herriman) a thing
imponderable as   justice.

Fidelity

"I don't know how to handle men.
I bring them on, I know I do.
I can't help that. And then — and then —
it isn't as if I wanted to —
but there they are in actual pain —
and often quite attractive, too.
So it happens again and again and again.

But basically I am true to you."

Recollection from the AAF (A Scatology)

How he'd blare (Beg pardon) "Horseshit!",
biting the "t" off flat
with a gambler's grin — the ref-
utation-ultimate,
the *reductio-ad-scat* —

I often remember now:
Dwyer, a flight-cadet
from Flatbush in Brooklyn —
which raised some question how
he'd seen a horse, even, let

alone the product invoked.
But its force was restorative —
so far a cry from the cold,

crowded, propellor-stroked
quads we learned war in. . . . Give

credit, then, for exot-
ic guanos never beheld
that littered the lost streets
of Dorado and Camelot
but nevertheless smelled;

for imaginary hip-
podromes with real turds
in them. . . . I can still see
that curled back upper lip
summoning shadowy herds

of Percherons, Clydesdales to
void on and inundate
some latest official in-
humanity or SNAFU. . . .
I miss their muster of late —

the Law a pissing-post
for liars, assassins. . . . *Hey,
Dwyer!*. . . . But he bought the farm
near Brest and enough compost
at last. So I'll quote, if I may. . . .

Equinoctial

I'm happiest sawing wood, I guess,
balanced there over the cut — as much
pull as push — as the blood goes —
from the heart, then toward it —
or the breath goes, or a fiddle bow.
We're at home somehow
where a balance is.

So much is out of reach:

The banties going to roost
in the lilac and apple branches,
the last light high up the hill,
the blue-grey and gold slow
soundless catastrophes of the clouds,
crows flying eastward,
the heart's desire . . . the mind's dominion . . .

What a relief
to speak what can hurt nobody:
"Crows from the north came early. . . ."
implying nothing, only
a hard winter and a difference
in crows (the winter ones
soaring more, cawing in flight more,
like ravens); and, to a sawyer, per-
haps that the years also
are sawed — into lengths and seasons
by a ragged alternation of black-
quilled rakers and cutters, rasping
to and fro, north and south.

Push and pull   push and pull,
half a yard only, my own
alternation goes. No talent's
required, only standing in one place. How much
more should one ask, though,
when whatever's gone is gone
and what is to come or not come nothing
can reach, and what we have
we have only on balance?

Themes for Pibroch

*The author humbly acknowledges debt to
the following persons now and again quoted or
pillaged without specific attribution in these
pages: Robert Frost, Richard Wilbur, Gerard
Manley Hopkins. Also to J.A. Baker — the
"Essex Man" in the text — author of "The Peregrine"
(Harper and Row, 1967).*

(Pibroch *is the Gaelic term for a formal
lament played on the highland bagpipe, or Col Mor. . . .
There is no music more rigorously — not to say
ferociously — governed by tradition.*

I
(Whales)

"She blows! . . . She blows! . . . " Of course
someone has to say it. . . . White puffs
exploding into the gale far out and fading
over wind-ivoried black-hackled ocean . . .
and then the low crescent of the whale, odd-
ly rigid against the tossing water,
like the rim of a slow wheel turning — its axle
steady as a meridian under
the seas' shuddering tons . . .

I came to marvel. And most
marvellous it is. Nevermind
that the naturalist aboard ship calls them
(the sea's creatures) "peleegic".
He does his best; but at *its* best, even,
the language would never touch them.
They'd as soon be mispronounced
as pronounced upon in it, whose own
language (we've learned) has no ambiguity more
than light has, simply carrying
the shapes and conditions of things, the plain
unvarnished sonar of each other
and the sea and all in it. No more
could they fib (or mispronounce)
than the sun could send forth shadows.

Even now, given three cetologists
for every whale — and how many harpooneers —
the whales that are left heave up
and blow and vanish as they have forever.

        I think of my father
striding in an odor of Edgeworth-and-leather

through the tame Westchester woods,
kids running to keep up, of a Sunday afternoon.

    "That's wild country up there," he'd say
of certain counties to the north
on his sales route. The word "wild,"
though for him not a seaward
but a landward term, nonetheless
signified some *mysterium tremendum*. And
because he was a spellbinder (not
a salesman for nothing) so
did it to us, and does still,
and comes to mind now in this
boundless forest of saltwater, wind and light. . . .

Thus it is with a dwindling of us
whose sires or grandsires were here
before the great continental wilderness withered
forever, and had felt its presence —
if only with a kind of holy dread —
whether they'd ever gazed on it or not.
Remembering them, we grow homesick
for a different distribution of things
between the human and non-human . . . Amps,
hot-dogs and all, then, we churn out
past the last lobster pots and the last buoys
in the wanhope of Job's and Ishmael's
Leviathan rising from the deep.

    And he rises —
he has to, to breathe. Amped at
and sub-chased every summer day
by fleets of excursioners, still
he rises. Or she: A cow finback
with her calf — concentric, flank against flank, two black
planets conjunct in the lens of the sea.

Banality itself — tourism — swirls
into nothing in the wash of a whale, its baleen
shooting a pale jade light through the waves at its forehead,
the sound of the vast vaporizing sigh
as it vanishes under a flukeprint
of imploding black water.

Then nothing for a while, "The sea's
slow miles of crumbling silence . . ."
The whale-watch watches itself
rising and falling,
not only to the sea's beat but also
to the thermals and downdrafts of one-
another's attention or indifference.
Basic primatology, one could say.
An entire society in microcosm
forming itself — all styles
and degrees of consciousness — whole
pods of ratiocinating grandmothers,
mothers, fathers, kids, newlyweds,
unweds, de-weds, and what others —
one with a highland bagpipe
for hailing the humpback whale.
(Legend has it the pipes palaver
with wild things; why not, then, with those
indefatigable symphonists of the abyss?)
And of him I could say, "There's me!"
if I had the snapshot — that one
with his passport of tasselled wood,
ivory and leather, who has just skirled
"The Gairdener's Childe" from the deck house
to a monster as resolutely mute
as the mud of the sea bottom.

Palisaded thus behind drones
and chanter, he is spared, as though

part of the crew, much routine social
and moral taxonomy.

But there's one grandmother aboard,
with the haggard's eye and horsey overbite
of Brahminical Yankeedom, who
measures him with an oblique look
at once wistful and critical
as though reminded of someone
she did not trust, or wished she hadn't. —
An event, in his private *polis*,
of equal magnitude to the breaching
of a twenty-ton finback calf a half-
mile off the bow. (All you can see,
in truth, is the splash, a momentary
nest of white foam in the feathering sea-race.
But the whale, says the loudspeaker,
hurled itself clear of the water.)

What grandmothers, landlocked or seafree,
need to know goes beyond costume
or occupation, straight
to the cosmic and phylogenetic: Age.
Marital status. It is still
written there in her face, something
being remembered, when the whale breached . . . .

So you see (Mr. Heisenberg)
how it is, how one mind aboard
has to factor in, beside whales
and grandmothers, an observor who,
with a certain pre-posthumous in-
delicacy, has left a wife.—
Not long since and for no reason
any fierce old Falmouth Eumenid
would listen to   even out here
on a blue cusp of the planet

plumed with the breath of leviathans
where there isn't a single fixed point
in the universe and no man is at home. . .

Least of all this one who climbs
once again to the wheelhouse
to blow back at the wind some
jumble out of *col mor* ancient
and monotonous almost
as the sea itself   from whose marbled
furrows the Humpback replies only
in his eponymous and promontorial shrug. . . .

II
(Peregrines)

Ashore and car-borne again, headed
roughly west-southwest from Wareham
and Cape Cod, considering the Humpback and Finback
on their alien and vaporous planet —
how the differently-colored water
at its head makes a baleen whale
seem a continent unto itself,
or an atoll, with submerged reef,
shallows, tidemark, skyline
steady above the waves . . . One can imagine
being *on* an island, hardly *being* an island.
Which of course is the death of him.
He can't hide. Not a whole geography.

Nor can we. Though we bulk less,
we seem to make more of a wake
than a whale — fifty years, say —
and everything on the record. . . . Hell,
we are all wake, and must live with it. —
And drive faster and faster, lest,
slowed down, we be overtaken
by a following wave. — Unlike
those trees there, epauletting
the road shoulder. They, for sure,
stand to be counted: Huge
lives lived in one spot . . . (They lift
their arms in bewilderment
at the traffic — all that
lateral velocity merely
to be parked somewhere else. . . .)

But it's already autumn. I mean
once more, if it's not too late,

to hail ". . . Kingdom of daylight's dauphin", that
cloud- and crag-haunter, *falco peregrinus. . . .*

> *"He is dying out they say —*
> *they say, not I. I, mind,*
> *who have never hooded or belled or flown*
> *falcon of any kind*
> *can't cancel him — subtract from sky*
> *sky's heart, that beating speck . . . ."*

                                        No,
nor *will* I. Nor will you, Tim,
whom we took on a walk once — seven
you were then — and showed a hawk overhead.
You followed it till it was lost
in a storm of light and cloud-chasms
over hills gilded and dim with distance,
then you said, more as if to it
than to any of us, "I hate people.
I wish I could be free like that."

I know how it is, Tim, having quaked,
half a century back, in that same
surprising scapular tug aloft,
with no way to answer, no out
from the multiple prisons of the flesh.
Yet I remember elation, not bitterness, glimpsing
so fabulous and majestic a dominion
(Seven leagues! Seven leagues at a lift
of those sunbeam stilts!)
There was a kind of glory even
in being denied it. . . . None perceived then
what "people" could do to a planet —
with our billions of little intellectual mandibles. Though
now every seven-year-old knows. Well,
come on, Tim, even so
you felt it, the totemic tug,

the shadow of Horus, hawk-god of the Pharaohs;
or that odd, bitter cry
had not been torn from you.
Even now at the world's end, then,
he is with us, anointing in wind
or light his unlikely hierophants.

    In England there is, or was,
one who for ten years, alone,
tramped the downs and cliff-brows of Essex
like a Majus, his star the wild peregrine.
He'd no wish to tame or possess, only
to be received, if might be,
into their wildness — and was once: A falcon
perched near him and preened, indifferent. He asked no more.

And Second Frederick of Hohenstaufen,
the Holy Roman Emperor,
was wont to forget his warlords on the Dneiper,
his tribute of kings, his castles and concubines,
to canter over the cold stubble, cloud-towarding,
and unfist the gyr and the peregrine,
like bolts back at the gods, tears in his eyes
for the untakeable heights.

Then a long fall to one
neither emperor nor anchorite,
alas, an old miser of time
and wastrel of all else,
failed, faithless again and again, save
to that same — say what it may — gale-
glorying, dawn-drawn Odysseus
in his white-isled Aegeans of air.

And thence to you, Tim, near twenty now.
Hardly what one calls old, only

it is late, late, and
the value to be placed on a single year
expands toward infinity. *Zoion
Holokausticon* has learned little since,
in the sign of Horus, you cried out
to be free of him, free of us.

      South-southwest and then South:
Cape May — and the call goes up,
"Peregrine". And all glasses swing
out toward the dunes where one comes
cart-wheeling and side-winding, black
in the sea's blaze, rings up
up up on a shaft of sea-light
to hang awhile with ospreys, accipiters —
at their height like a hatch of moths
migrating to the moon, so many,
funnelled here in the west wind; then
he dives, like a meteor, at a mourning dove,
passes it by, beats southward again   is gone.

No mistaking the glory, the fierce joy. He flies
the way you or I would fly
were we to awake one morning, the rainbow
wings of a Fra Angelico angel
fitted to our shoulders.

But what would our falco-phile
recluse of Essex make of Cape May
in autumn, where a thousand raptorial birds,
the odd peregrine among them,
can pass overhead in an hour? Rarity's,
after all, what we ask of them —
what we ask of everything, wary
at the heart's hard exchequer
of too-easy interest. Back in Essex

the hawk, though with no economics, no
esthetic, comprehends rarity; has
to be rarity itself, or starve; wherefor
the epiphanic long fall, the bolt,
once in a lifetime, out of a bland blue
blank, cherub'd with steepling pigeons.

The pigeons at Cape May are tethered,
and flung to tree-height from a blind —
hawk-bait at the banding station.

A place of *lèse-majesté*,
one would guess, to our Essexman,
where raptors shoved into tubes
lie on tables like bunches of celery
awaiting their bin marks.

Then they're let go (It is not
". . . ungentle, only thoroughly departmental.")
with the bander pronouncing on peregrines:
". . . Really a stupid bird. We'll catch
the same tiercel four times. . . ."

I did not ask him
whether, in his opinion,
nature corrupts men
or men corrupt nature

(or whether the question only
un-asks itself, an *en-*
antidromion). But
the idea of that tiercel
turned loose and looming again
to tree height and folding for the same dive
into the same net, as helpless

104

to comprehend nets as a tentworm
to comprehend freedom — while
his first swerve out of wilderness
into civility wins him
a leg-iron for life. . .Isn't there
a tale the obverse of his,
concerning bands on the mind,
and nets — the nets of judgement,
of blood and custom, of meaning-
against-unmeaning—and whether
we are ever out of them?

III
(Clara)

I knew
a nymph once — nymph
in the mayfly sense at least
of a phase, an aqueous phase,
preceding adulthood. . . . Nymphs
of the *ephemeridae*,
indeed, she half lived among,
apter to swim than walk,
as though brookwater, headlong
heedless and mercurial,
were in truth her element. . . .Nymph,
then. Or nymph enough, short
of the immortal. . .She was twenty-odd. . . .

In another May-month it was,
if lilac and rock-bell and jonquil
and warblers teetering
in the gilt tips of the maples — if
these made a Maytime when
by the bones' almanac and the Doomsday Clock
it was coming on to be Last Solstice — if
such could be a Maytime, then
Maytime it was in that year,
my greybeard fifty-first,
when I sat on the stone stoop
of an eyebrow-windowed house
built in John Quincy Adams' time
(and last painted in LBJ's)
squinting into the sun
and the double cul-de-sac
of old age and Armageddon,
and a red pickup truck came a-swagger
down the dirt road with a load of mulch hay

and Clara, the Clums' new milker, at the wheel,
her hair like an avalanche of brass rings, bright
even in the shadow of the cab, and the sheer
historical impudence of it
overwhelmed the gloom I'd been in
and the girl braked and yelled up
   "Tough life you have! Where's your wife?"

   "Mercy-calls," I yelled back
(And without hyperbole. A kettle
of hot soup was en route
to somewhere — the webs and shackles
of this world worn, by one at least,
with a grace that made garlands of them. . . .)

   "She shames the saints," the girl said.
"Where's she want this hay?"

We piled it north of the garden,
some thirty bales; and as if
each one were a year off my back
I'd forgotten by the end of it
all but what warblers or hawkweed —
or a herd-girl in her twenties — knew
of what May meant, what arms meant
when they'd meet sometimes, sweaty,
rank with hay-mould. . . . It was hot,
and the brook was high then,
a heavy jade-grey
crush of cold water jamming
through it from the late rains, and
with the last bale still settling it seemed,
we were both at the trout-lie
and the girl in it, nude as a naiad,
unabashed, breasts bobbing,
thighs glass-smooth, occluded
and dense as the crowded water. . . .

The thing seemed — the thing *was*—
impossible — though it came
as close to *athlos,* perhaps, as to *eros* —
a body in conscious and full function
flung first at a freezing cataract
then at a man, as though
in successive field-events.

    And if any man, since Adam,
could have fished for tobacco then
and talked of other things,
let angels praise him. I could contract
to be twenty again   or throw
at least, a salute to the old maples
with their new leaves in their arms. . . . As if
the elixir of the Impossible
weren't poured in this world only
to annihilate — like anti-
matter against matter.

                        But why
it was poured ever, first or last,
Clara never said   or only
that the "wailing" of bagpipes
made her "lonesome as the moon". . . . And yes,
sometimes, to the mere blowing-in
of the drone reeds, wouldn't Clara
come glimmering out of the green tide
of a top-heavy hayfield
like a *silkie* out of the surf?. . . No question
a wildness in her answered
a wildness in them . . . .

    "There *we* go!" she said once,
watching two cabbage butterflies
spiraling into the summer zenith. . . .

But there's no *Vita.* Nothing
but the odd datum, and not much

108

other-worldly in that: Cheerleader,
prom queen, suburbia,
apostasy to an Ag school,
a milker's and mucker's job
and none to be stunned at the sight of her
but two rows of holstein rumps
because, by a freak un-conjunction
of planets, she was never *Discovered*
and lifted — another celluloid
Andromeda — into the stars? — No,
it doesn't explain much.
If any words could. But leave it
for one who can wet water
or burn fire   to clarify Clara.

Granting of course each eye
brings its own coordinates
to the locus of beauty, still
by whatever calculus, women
and men both brightened
at how Clara'd come on — not
wearing but *being* a taunting
coral-and-white smile curled
up on one side, dimpling
a cheek like a nectarine's, hair
a corona — banners blowing
in their own wind — and a flesh
surfaceless, trading itself off softly
everywhere into light. . . . Words, even,
from her were mesmeric. Clara's
"Fifty cents," (I can still remember
her frown of bewilderment
when urged twice to repeat it)
was kitchen-theatre: the lips'
lingering flare on the "f",
the alignment behind them of white teeth
on "cents", the insistent chin thrust

forward and touching with a flicker of scorn
the final sibilant. . . . Yet

above all   when I think of Clara
it's her sweet breath I remember,
the odor of warm milk that came from her,
or of moss and brook-water. — *Spiritus
Clarae*, one could say — the Latin
comes closer. She seemed,
for all her confessed waywardness, free
of some fundamental taint — the fetor
of bad teeth, bad digestion, bad conscience —
and to live by some in-
stinctual hermaneutics
day to day for two years
an Arcadian *Now*, guiltless
as the waves of the sea are
in whatever comes to toss
on their hollows and swells   or parasitize
or their cleansing oblivion — seeing
nothing is promised, nothing exacted. . . .

After she'd gone — with less trace
it seemed, than the shadblow — and anti-
marriage had annihilated
marriage   and like old Rip
in the Catskills I'd waked up
in the future   and it was all rust
and cobwebs   and even these
shaken by voices in the air,
apocalyptical voices,
crying we'd come too far,
sunlight was cancerous, brook-
water dangerous to drink —
what came then was an odd
paralysis of regret —

110

regret itself broken
like a board over a stone
between a wildness lost
and a steadiness lost.

It was then, in that bleak lucidity, in-
different as firmament, those
archetypical images —
Great Whale, Wandering Falcon—
arose — and as more than image:
as symbol: verbs in that lost Ur-
logos that ordained the Earth.

Could they still exist? — In this
twilight of nature, twilight
of self, the world turning
into a metaphor
on the impossibility of innocence? . . .

 . . . and then that I drove east
to search for mind in the waters
and 'crossbows in the clouds'

and one day, perhaps, pipes willing,
penetrate the arcane *pibroch*
and sound the archaic long
droning discordant bittersweet
Da Capos of defiance and lament,
for the nets of blood and custom
and the hawk's freehold and the whales'

and the white butterflies spiraling
into their summer zenith. . . .

New Things
Come into the World

Christmas Figures (Chatham, N.Y.)

I look out over half an acre
of tarmac and a gas station
to St. James', where the big bell
clamors nine times in its tower
of red sandstone, scattering pigeons,
gathering families, in blues, greens, vermillions
that blink out in the vestibule
like toys tumbled into a box;

and further on, the late shoppers
crowding both sides of the street,
each storefront a little glacier
calving white parcels, to bob
in the pedestrian torrent . . .

From a secular point of view,
the thing is astounding: A thousand
townspeople, particulate
and at odds otherwise, now moving
together in one wave, obeying
(as it were) new equations required
by the multiple reappearance along
Main Street of the Holy Family,
the camels and coffers of the Magi.

Much-improving with distance, these
effigies mercifully recede
toward a vanishing-point one might
imagine as approached in time
rather than space: A recession
of Christmases toward the First
Christmas, as though you looked
down the barrel of a telescope,

from the wrong end, and could see it —
"the distant and anterior point,"
Time-Zero, inhabited
by minuscule but familiar figures
in unconscious and honest aureoles.

But, seen or imagined, they're there; that is
not only on the courthouse lawn
in non-bio-degradable plastic,
or again in the hairdresser's window,
but *there*, at the origin, by
very nomenclature of time,
by *Christ* and by *Christian Era*; there
where the ordinals of our days

begin, where we start counting
solstices, gasping up now
to one thousand, nine-hundred
and eighty-odd . . . But although
the faces look straight at us
up the long Zodiacal tunnel,
we are hidden from them
in our blind of tinsel and holly,
of Christmases-out-of-mind.

They know nothing of Christmas —
two saints yet-to-be and a god
not a night old. Nonetheless
it is what they *are*. No one
in this town, though he forget
the names of the emperors, popes,
nations — or even of his own
neighbors — can forget these
that attach — of all things! — to the sacrament
of selflessness, to the giving of gifts
and the adoration of innocence.

So the hairdresser buys her nephew
a toy submachine-gun; and the judge
sinks enough for a poor boy's tuition
into lights for his spruce trees; and
Sinatra, dreaming of his white
etcetera, turns it to slush;
and Peter is false three times;
and Christian history is two
thousand annals of vanity
and whited sepulchres. . . . And all
spiral around one homely
paradigm of beatitude. . . . Christ,

we don't notice till we get old,
and time foreshortens, how
there was this form to it after all,
how indeed there could be no history,
as there could be no speech,
absent such principle — a *grammar*,
without spatial coordinates
yet containing all that's prescribed,
permissible — making coherent:
Europe, The West, from Augustus
to the Sunbelt Republicans;
all appeals to perfection going —
though they go to the sound of gunships
and bullhorns — even so, going
to the still center, to Selflessness.

Now we pass it in perigee. This
is as close as we come, and yearly
the spiral is wider. No one
is uncrossed, them least of all
who were truly gentle — the Son-
of-Mary, say, or the Right Whale — no creature
and no thing, the planet itself
perishing of its man-plague. And

for all that, I can't bear
to sit here alone, am glad
I can pull on my own coat
and walk along *crêche* street, repeating
Merry Christmas Merry Christmas
and not be thought mad.

Lines for a Birthday

Dear ———,
     To whom else could I mention
the Pleiades' reappearing now
at nightfall? . . . I know.
They are not *your* stars. But those
are in Sagittarius, opposite,
where the sun is, an hour ago
swallowed up like a high-fly-ball
in the Oligocene Stone mitt
of the mountains across the river. You
could never have seen them,
or seen any stars till these,
brightening in the east, brought on
the first night you were here. . . . The Pleiades . . .
The Seven Sisters . . . I wonder
if you know that old tale: The Seven
flying from the wrath of Orion
the Huntsman in his *traje de luce*,
his belt and his sword
and his bonnet of lights, right behind them —
and all of them changed into stars

so that the flight and pursuit, the fugue,
goes on forever and forever. . . .

But I think something was wrong
in the version I learned. Wrath,
even hatred, couldn't last that long.
Only longing could, which is why,
surely, there is such a word. . . .

We've learned what it means, though,
again and again, haven't we? —
If not why we had to,
or why the whole universe
seems to be torn in two
between what it is and would be.

I'll tell you what I think: It's so,
to give Forever something to do:
Far way there on the night sky
separating the giants in the stars;
down here in the dust, us,   and whatever
we're running from, or toward.

Laundry off Fire-Escapes

It's one of the few things we do
to advantage: deploy in line
of piping-white, scarlet and blue
blouses, trousers and tunics   dressed-
left and dressed-right   our
fresh-scrubbed replacements. Their
order, though come from us,
is so much superior to ours
it seems they'd do better without us
from now on. I believe they would.

It is not meant to look pretty —
which of course is one reason it does —
that high-flown way they form front
like cherubs and angels-militant
among their own scrolls and gonfalons.
We can only tear that down:
Blood/mud/manure/gravy   the in-
disciplines of the dust.

A pity.

A Point of Origin

I looked ahead to my life then.
It seemed to await me somewhere
to the west, over that whalehump
of a hill on the horizon and grandly
alluded to in a stunned splendor
of cumulus Corinths and Camelots. . . . Now,

here I stand again. And, oddly,
the now-ness of this Now, fifty
years after, feels just the same
as the first Now. . . . I think there is nothing
but Now, and we surf on it. . . . Or
that time is like Treasury paper, a
deficit passing current, sure
to smother us in the end. . . . I think:
Half a century blown, and what's bought?
Some pride, but as much regret.
And these, too, soon to be spent.

And less splendor in the whole of it
than in one hour of those dazzling, immense
cordilleras of mock-marble, building
into a blue August zenith,
without history and without intent.

Time Travel (Route 91 at Night)

To travel in time — revisit
the Past — it would be like this,
I suspect, or this is it:

the crouching, encapsulated
in metal and glass, the speed,
the enormities of the hills
by moonlight and cloud-march, un-
altered in all history and so
close we could almost touch them,
or they us . . . But we move too fast.

There can be no communication. If
they reach out — with a moth, say,
or a fox — it vaporizes
against our reality; and
if we swerve into them it's we
who explode instead. And still

we see it there. A grave darkness
platemarks the Past for us. We don't
allow that in our time; the lights
never black out. Inside
each capsule, tachometers glare
and, outside, our highbeams and tail-lights
bring a full moon to naught.

                    The huge
and unbroached casks of blackness
looming from the river and road-cut
westward — a wilderness, un-
interested in revolutions
per minute or millennium — they

are like the name of the place:
Northeast Kingdom . . . Northeast
Kingdom . . . I can hear Joubert:

"The republic is the only cure
for the ills of the monarchy; the
monarchy, for the ills of the republic."   We
don't outdistance that gentle despair,
though we drive ever so fast.

The one cure for the Past is the future;
the one cure for the future, the Past.

A Wild Place

The sky is a wild place — if
you could call it a place, what
with every point in it approaching
or fleeing some other. Sky
is without fixity and un-
welcoming; yet we long for it,

a condition of drifting cloud,

as though we'd prefer space
to time — for there's none there:
Whatever is, *is*, for an instant
so microchrone the word "now"
manages it like a back-
hoe picking a bluet,

then *is not*, the nephelographer's
atlas forever void. Oh yes,

I remember (far back) an entire
'Empyrean' — a summer storm
self-destructing toward dusk
in Himalayan masses of rose-
quartz, tourmaline, ivory —
and the whole photographed in a lake
so still you could see a fish flop
half a mile out. Oh yes,
I've never forgotten. But
all it meant to do was vanish,
instant by instant — and so did
that I've wondered often by what
provenience we infringe
on a cosmic obliviousness,
presume to remember a thing.

Can it be that the very old — those
of whom we'd say *She is going* or
He doesn't know us anymore —
were slightly mixed up with sky
already, were turning to weather?
I can believe now they were.
Gone wild — the space they were in
no longer particular but
as fugitive to all logic as
the locus of an electron. . . . Oh,
it was wild over the lake that evening!
And, after, the stars in their own slow
storm of silence and light . . . There it stops.
I was sent off to bed, I guess. —
But to wild dreams, surely. Surely
wildness waits at the end.

November and Shakespeare

That wan, open look the woods have —
glaucous, old-bronze, grey-black,
like the bare grate
after October's wildfire (while
rectangular fields, in their mock-Spring,
riot in the frosty light,
greener than ever). . . . Inevitably
it comes to mind: "That time of year
thou mayst in me behold . . ."
                              Only
I for one wouldn't go from here
to a plea for love — for those
wild scarlets and yellows again. . . . No,
beyond all those, it seems,
there was this cold clarity
everything aimed at, although
no more aware of it then
than exempt from it now.

Notes on Extrospection

That we need to look at the world
through something . . . Not straight on,
unmediated . . . A smoke,
an arch, a window, a line of trees,
a trajectory of birds — something
between one and the horizon
with its vanishing-points, its end-
of-the-world implications . . . Or
words — better amorous
and merry, for sure — but even
words only trying, like these,
to flag with some metaphor
what we can't compass, what we
are encompassed by: a karma
of exploding eternities, the
further out we can see
the less to do with us . . .

Night Thoughts

One could easily believe time
patienter than it is, indeed
that it stands still, nights
when there's no wind   and it's hot
and a misshapen moon
like a clinker out of a forge smolders
in the dun discard of the sky.

Say it's three a.m. and
you're still half in some dream
condensing a lifetime's terror and despair,
and there's no sound.
And it seems things will remain so
forever — because *nothing moves*,
nothing, neither moon nor cloud
nor a single peripheral star
among all the maples' opaque
galaxies (as if this were it,
the dread amber: one had entered
the past — the unalterable). . . . I am glad

I saw or felt once, looking west
at dusk, that the sun wasn't
going down behind hills
but the hills rising,
grandly, like a ship's rail, up up
till they blocked all light,
looming above us — one
vast black irregular gunwale — then
over, somersaulting us —
silos, highways and towns — headfirst
into the dark, to hang there in-
explicably not tumbling away down
into Draco and The Dipper. It

doesn't stand still, I mean.
The hills even now are clambering
at a thousand miles an hour
to smother that red ember of a moon
under such an avalanche, I
might even find an hour's peace afterwards somewhere,
or you a glimmer of romance.

Earth Tremor

But it had a *beat*. A fixed rhythm.
Not one like music's exactly;
more like an immense crankshaft's
to whose humdrum thrust evey bulk-
head in a ship shudders
as a sea heaves the screws clear.

Like that, like feeling a moment
whatever engines those are,
fired by hell's boilers four thousand
miles down, driving us, dragging
a wild skiff of a moon. . . . Some sudden
tsunami in time, or a 'gravity-wave'
warping us bows-under, foam
to the forehatches? Who knows? But
it's the beat, the measured beat
that talks to us. Lord, it's all
some of us understand, making —
well, if not music exactly —
the joint jump, the floor shimmy. . . . Praise

be, then, for that manifest
piston or heart or drum
or prosody in the bedrock
and roll of the world that only
whispered to us, spared us this time
the ultimate amplifier.

Footnotes

Now I've seen a brown hornet light,
six points, on a puddle   and sit
dimpling the surface, not
breaking it,   and a breeze blow him
clear-across   like an iceboat.
Then he buzzed back to windward
and tried it again. Three times
he lit and was wafted
on his hair skates.   Will you tell me
it was not a game —
and moreover not just then invented?

New things come into the world. I watched
a crow overhead once — a one-
bird barnstorm: He'd hold
a scrap of hide in his bill,
and again and again drop it —
and then in a drunken swoop
snatch it back out of the air
with his claws — against all the laws
of ornithology.

And you too will remember,
though it seem sad now,
how once in the resinous dusk
under summer hemlocks a chickadee
rustled down from a twig and
(whatever he thought we were)
like a small grey priest
joined us together, perching
on our clasped hands.

A Downed Butterfly

Yet here it is. This is *meant*
and is no accident. (How
speak of 'design-by-
accident' and not stultify
English?) One can allow

being whacked by a windshield
in mid-hover and killed. *That*
is accident. But not this,
every index of artifice
in its mesmeric format,

and artifice far beyond
any we understand: Two
red-orange smouldering
discs on each dun wing
like planets, one in full view

the other occluded. — What
on earth do we make of it? I
already imagine things —
like harp-shaped shadowy wings
wide as the night sky

and rimmed in such blues
and ivories and rainbows, such
astronomies! — and that sure-
ly God looks a lot more
like this than like us.

Things at a Distance

Physics can't compass this:
how the land, far off there,
falls away westward, hill
behind hill, immaterial
with distance, azure as air;
the fact, I mean, that it *is*

immaterial, in the sense
(sight) that the entire
blue tumult enters the mind
instantly, that we find
the space — or it doesn't require
space, having no substance;

nor can words, our terrible need
sometimes for this aliment
that depends on or is distance:
its pure forms, its silence,
and extinction of incident,
its nature-to-intercede. . . .

"Why is it we leave always
what we love most?" The thought,
so far from the sick heart
of the case, can become art;
God knows, the goodbyes were not.
In distance. Distance. Such grace.

Some Small Bird

Some small bird out there —
a titmouse I think —
saying *chee-ew   chee-ew* . . . Likely
it is not at all sad. Likely
it is just that none answers
so the call is alone there
in the whole of the morning
with its faint up-lilt at the end
that would make it a plea, if
you or I said it: *where-*
are-you, where-are-you, or
is that not my love out there
in the breakers, that brown speck . . .

I like how a bird's cry
has no parts of speech
but is speech itself —
and is not about anything; no,
everything else is about it.   Listen.

Sun blinding on snow

bare limbs

an enigma

a solitude

"O"

I will dial the zero then,
the bubble, call-letter of foam,
and see if Aphrodite answers
or someone calling me home

or the Captain of the Whales. . . . How
many phones are unlisted there
in the restricted venues
of crusted carronades
and spilled *moidores.* . . .

I've a friend who owns one.
Bought at the border. Beautiful
spiral white horn. Cordless. Dial-less.

Pick it up and you hear a sound
with the whole of the sea in it —
the sonars of the whales quaking
the lengths of meridians,
the day of the Foam-Born
when the tides turned salt with tears;

the prolonged monosyllable
of Time — that   NOW
whose   O   is the turning world.

NYC Vignettes

I (Broadway at 104th)

A heavy-faced man
in a brown suit. No tie.
Nineteen-forties fedora. He sees
a little wizened balloon —
a green one —
like a winding-down butterfly,
or a frog, perhaps, stuffed with buckshot,
unable to rise   but *trying*
to rise — a faint
erectility there in the ditch — the
literal last gasp
of somebody's party. . . . This guy
detours to and stomps on it. Then
nothing's left, just a green smear,
and he moves off, muttering. . . .
                              What

do you say to an act like that?
(*So O.K., Mister, O.K. —*
Party's over. You satisfied?
For Christsake, next time wear a tie!)

A poor downed and de-tumefying
pucker of a thing that still,
for better or worse, had breath in it? I
couldn't quite overhear the mutter —
but know there are things men want
they don't *want* to want. . . . Wilde, surely,
would have recognized this guy
who does it with a kick

and in the gutter.

II (Washington Square Park)

Hi-tech? I'll give you hi-tech:
Six kids with a transistor-
radio, all-chrome, dazzling
as death and Christmas . . . Lit
up like the instrument deck
on an AWAC bomber . . . Volume
way over the pain-line . . . (People
must hear it in Hoboken.) . . . Top
Hard-Rock Punk Porno Hit . . .
Girl vocalist vooming: *Mista,*
what is that thang? It look
like a fire extinguisha!. . . .

With mobile bottoms and im-
mobile faces, the future,
The Second Coming,
dances to it.

Glimpse of a Better Way

To get above grief, to use it —
that leaden will-of-its-own
to crush the life under it — use it
for a launching pad, toss
into the sun from it . . . O,
if only it could be done . . .

What about that bird
that wanders a thousand mile
and never once touches down,
that Albatross . . . .

Tops of Trees

The trees top out
and from there on it's sky —
the same sky everywhere
the same trees even;
or the same gesture: Goodbye

as if someone or something
had gone, and had left them there
pointing after it, waving perhaps. . . .
Oh sure, it would be the wind
if they did that. There's no
transaction at all, you can say.

But there is one, with the eye —
drawn upwards and then let go
to such utter treelessness
the next hard object's the moon
and if you miss that, nothing.
A Torque. An Eternity. True,
it's nothing to them. They can stand it.

At best, we might under-stand it.
But once, stopping alone
in a featureless town,
I looked up, in a cleft
where a few trees grew,
and had to look back down
to see if I'd anything left.

Getting It

It seemed to have something to do
with growing old — or —
no — admitting to oneself
there must be all kinds of men
at each moment, and therefor
some age'd, faded and poor
whom no Helen ever again
will immortalize-with-a-kiss
(if any ever did). . . . Yes,
that was it: Even if, even so,
something else was astir then,
which doesn't let up or let go,
recommence, or forget.

The nudge of recognition in that.

Like the flash of one burst star
in the Magellanic Cloud
that kept coming and coming
for thousands of years, forever
and ever, straight at us —
and even so
never arriving, never remotely
imagined. But here now.

Enlightenment

Agreed. We're born knowing (although
not yet knowing we know)
and all learning must touch —
indeed, must elicit —
what we knew already;   the rest
just slips by!. . . . A credit,
unique in each case,
of anterior axioms — such,
in the cells, then, underlies
every human face. . . .

I remember a sudden bright
smile — vacant, inane, arch-
aic — like flowers. . . . The world
was made for pleasure, it said.
Of course I knew otherwise.
Always. But oh, that light —
what could enlighten it!

Gossip

What I reckon now is:
He was lucky. Oh, not
in the ultimate loss,
but the sheer sum of it —
having that to forfeit.

Old Fool, you will say —
Old Fool that he was
for the slant of an eye
and the swirl of a dress
and the swell of a blouse. . . .

Oh, granted. But this
you can't take away:
that he sojourned in bliss
for a year and a day
come what may, come what may.

In Defense of Old-Fashioned Rhetoric

Why, what a thing's *like* matters
above all else! As for me,
before looking up just now
deep into those gold, overlaid
masses of maple leaves

I'd but half known how your hair
lifted and filled with light
one summer day by the sea.

Something

Yet something insists to us
that the world is beautiful.
(Would I not have written
that whole book of Von Rezzori's
just to say, ". . . a turquoise sky was taking
a step into the universe"?)

Mathematical Statement

Intellect, Passion, Morality = Scissors, Paper, Rock

On "The Mathematics of Chaos"

As to Chaos — and also
to the riddle of Time — clouds
are instructive: Ourselves
evidently in synchrony
with someting in them, as they crumble
and fray (from a horse in a capriole
to a swan's wing), we stare at
but can't quite detect
the process, say *when*
the horse vanishes,
the tossed mane and tail
become wing, then emptiness. Here's
the tempo at which boys bulge
into men, or men wizen, or History
sinks into sand. We can't
intervene here, it seems, our very
intervention its furtherance. What
of the self, then? Does this change?
No. I am ready to swear
I have watched over fifty years
with the same sweet insouciance
white clouds and time flying. . . . But
no matter. I'm willing to admit:
in a perfect Chaos, all things,
even constancy, love, grace
must occur — so illimitable
would be the Indifference.

The Way of Her

    It was like clear water
or like clean air:
No particular taste to it,
no odor, no color, nowhere
anything put up in front or in back of it,
so you saw clean through
and never knew it was there.

Until it was taken away
and you knew at once you'd begun
dying for lack of it.

"Bajazet"

A friend (better him than me)
has an old turkey. One.
A goitrous bird, the head
like a loading-hook
from a drowned galleon, cal-
careous with corals and whelks; feathers
a dun desert of dandruff and lice;
fan like a shattered snowfence; and feet
two blasted elm stumps. (It doesn't
walk, it uproots — first one
then the other.) Nevertheless,
it gobbles, it totters, erects
its toothless-smile of a tail, all
by itself in the dust and mulch-hay.

But to what end, then, or for whose
pleasure, the production? I
confess tenderness on the point,
likewise confronting an audience
unseen, hypothetical, such
audience as the castaway
sends to — his map-in-a-bottle. . . .

Behold!   (he is saying)   *I'm here!*

And the wind takes it away,
and the light. . . . It makes me proud
somewhat for old "Bajazet",
that antique — no matter alone
and the last gobbler on earth —
still ruffling his forlorn duster
and croaking his four trochées
to all the turkeys that ever were
in this world, or could be.

Cabin Company

They're a kind of company — im-
personal but not un-
interesting: the deep cold,
the dark, the violence of the wind's
percussive and atonal sym-
phonics, the cloud-mass dim-
lit from behind by the moon.

An America wild still!
Not peopled. Not paved from here
to the Pacific. Or not yet . . .
Even so, sometimes I wish . . .
But who would I not do ill
to wish this on — a hill,
a wild night, an old Lear?

At a Statue of Hamilton

Knowing more than they knew,
knowing everything, really, or
more than we want to know,
we dismiss them now, in their waistcoats,
their hose, their grandiloquence. If
we see them at all in our minds,
it's a kind of stage-play, a costume
and period-piece. They Strike
Attitudes, Gaze-Afar-
Into-The-Future.

They don't see us there.
Wouldn't know us if they did. . . . Still,
who could help striking attitudes
when every right-foot-advanced
broached the New Millennium;
and who would not Gaze-Afar
when all the History there was
he had written that morning: "A-little-
corruption-is-a-necessary-engine-
of-government." . . . Oh say,
Mr. Hamilton, can't you see —
Afar, of course — through the bronze
and the bird's dung — a Trail of Tears,
a Slaughter in The Wilderness,
A Gilded Age   an Empire
a Poisoning of the Earth
an Apocalypse? — You, aloft there
with the one foot advanced, the Gaze
infinite, leading the way.

"Mind in the Waters"

*"This is the mind I have always
believed existed somewhere."* — Joan McIntyre

The mystery of it is
we *do* recognize it
from somewhere —
from the womb perhaps, where we,
too, floated frictionless,
weightless, wantless, without
locus. . . . Or we once really believed
in the Beatitudes — once,
like the whales, might have looked with pity
on our trackers and torturers —
succored them, wished them well.

Or we loved something once
and should have died for it.

But the whales are heathen —
or are gods themselves. And still
even the last of them half-
seem to cooperate
in their own Gotterdammerung. So
it must be that *that mind,*
though the whole ocean is in it
and the keel of the planet quakes
to its bells and kettledrums, that mind
simply cannot conceive of ours.

You wonder what can — what did —
conceive ours — that only goes on
and on with the butchery
and the bleaching of bones, while,
for all we know, it is grieving for us
we hear in our hydrophones.

The Greenpeace Mariners

"Ah, love, let us be true to one another . . . ."
       — Matthew Arnold in "Dover Beach"

You almost wish they weren't there
sometimes, those peace-pirates or Mad
Mercyists you can't place either
with the terror or the counter-terror,
with the violent or the inert;
in fact can't place anywhere
outside of La Mancha
or the Mount of Olives. I swear
sometimes I'd rather be left,
like Richard in the play, to "that
sweet way I was in to despair",
seeing the end coming, seeing
five billion of anything nec-
essitous as men are
couldn't help conquering the world; seeing
how history, all unaware,
headed for this and it's here —
the sea-beaches blackened with dead
dolphins and pelagic birds;
disaster at Bhopal, the Rhine,
Chernobyl, the Three-Mile-Island,
the Love Canal. . . .

                 Ah love,
let us be true to one another. . . . Ah,
more, even: obsessed, oblivious
to the rest that we can't bear!

And still, those ridiculous
"far-distant, storm-beaten ships . . ."
No, not those of old Mahan,
looming between the Grande Armée

and the dominion of the world,
but little one-lungers that bob
on a bilge-pump and a prayer
between the harpoons and the whales,
  and between the ocean itself
and a sea-fill, a sewer — and at last
between history-as-horror and
history as honor. . . . Ah, love,
what could we, even,
promise to one another,
if they weren't there?

Trash

I suppose they're the trash of thought —
dreams. The mind's midden . . . Like
Poindexters, we "process a lot
of material"; the residue
has to go somewhere. Our oldest
waste-problem, is it not? —
Stuff unbecoming or im-
politic or un-
bearable to remember. Stuff
we thought we were rid of but
here it is still   in the dig
of deep sleep. Sometimes
not so deep, either. Sometimes
not asleep, even: the dream
thrusting up into sunlight — one
corner, at least, like an iceberg's,
or a tusk from a tar-pit,
or a damning memorandum. . . .

I helped a friend clean out a barn
a while back: Surprise for his wife
who was off visiting . . . So would I
be off visiting   if I lived
neighbor to that barn. A vom-
itorium it was, a charnel house,
a gigantic tumor, a hidden reef
whole decades had split on and foundered
and written the wrecks of their histories
in rot, rust, dung, dead chickens, rats,
rags, maggots, mildew and spilth from dirt floor
to roof joists and from hay-mow
to rafters. For five days Alan and I
dug there, damp cloths to our faces —
and still coughing — and five times

trucked six-and-a-half-ton loads
to the town dump.

                    "Our Mary
is one of those *savers*," he explained.
"Wouldn't throw away half a shoe
if the pig had eaten the other half. . . . But,
as you see, it got away from us." (I
sneezed and agreed.) "It's a paradox,"

he went on, in a series of parentheses
between coughs. "In everything else,
neat as a nuthatch. . . . I've mentioned
The barn a few times — as who wouldn't —
and she says, 'Oh, I'll get to that.
please! Leave it. Just leave it.
I know what I want to do down there.'

So I took to avoiding the place —
systematically, more or less —
and literally for years. . . . And now *this*!
Critical mass! Flash-point! Ground-zero!. . . ."

So we coughed and we dug   and we dragged
and we shovelled   and felt ashamed
at the waste-wake we leave in the world
and never look back at, till some
stoppage occurs   and the stuff
mucks up halfway to the moon
and we see we could drown in it — in-
deed are half drowned already. . . .

Five hundred old plastic half-gallon
empties the color of phlegm . . . Christ, yes!
To the Dump! (But what then,
when the dump's full? When a thousand
scowloads of filth wallow the coastlines

forever, forbidden to dump or dock —
a sea-full of *Flying Drekmen!*)

   Some weeks later we met,
and I asked about Mary. His face fell.
"She broke down and cried," was his answer.
"Accused me of treachery,
of going behind her back. Now
she's talking divorce. . . ."

                              (What was this?
I thought I knew Mary, knew her
as all did: a gracious, radiant,
competent, kindly soul; the sort
young and old take their troubles to.)
"God, Alan, d'you think she's all right?"
I broke in. "That doesn't make sense!"
"It does in a way," he mumbled.
"When you know the whole story."

And then he told it. Since when
I have thought much about dreams,
how they reach down, down
into whatever we've been,
and believed utterly buried

or burned   or shredded. . . .
                    "Years back,"
Alan said, "I went over the fence.
Got obsessed with another woman.
Mary knew, but she never reproached me.
She simply went on being Mary.
You know her. Chickadees on her shoulders . . .
That gentle luminousness
that seems more than half magic,
considering the world we're in. . . ."

(There was a break then,
Till he got his voice back.)
"But that, though I didn't mark it,
was where it began — the *saving.*
I see it now: From then on,
she couldn't let *anything* go — rags,
cans, cartons. . . . One part, I think,
was just having lost so much,
by her lights, already: Marriage.
What marriage meant; what it could
and should be. — I'd seen to that. —
But another part, and the part
nobody, not even Mary,
saw, until now, was rage:
a rage so relentless, consuming,
you or I'd have gone mad with it. . . .
But if Mary did, well,
she'd her own way to deal with it:
Simply, put madness aside —
in the barn there — let it grow
bottle by bottle, wad by wad, into a hell
of rottenness and reproach. . . . I'm afraid
what we hauled that week to the dump
was the thirty-some tons of ballast
Mary needed to go on being Mary,
go on as though all were well
and the marriage hadn't been trashed —
as she saw it — as I guess it had been. . . .

The absolute horror, I mean,
of that barn was for me to live with
if I lived with her.   My penance.

And now it's gone."

    What could I say? What *will* I say
next time we meet — if we do meet;

if he isn't gone, too, by this time? —
That he makes himself too important;
something else might lie underneath
that awful tumulus of trash
and demoralization? A woman
might shrewdly suppose such. But
what I think of now is the Admiral
(we'd had the Joint Hearings on
the whole time) and the hero's welcome
they gave him back home — no matter
the stake they had in that trash
he got rid of. But They *never knew*,
of course. Never even dreamed.

Histories Natural and Otherwise

I (The Sharp-shinned Hawk)

The day's news like a harpoon
broken off in my head —
Death Terror Deluge — I walked
crosslots and at random, hoping
to shake out. And instead
a small hawk shot past me,
flat, fast, like a missile
fired out of the sun,
and the next instant was gone
into the tree-line. Death
to something in there . . .

So: death again, even
'in the peace of the late afternoon' —
when, if you were a hawk, back-lit
and fast-moving, nothing could see you
to save itself. Neither could I
help a quick catch-in-the-breath
at the dash of it, the tactical
beauty: the blue bolt
loosed at a precise instant
and dead-on.   And no mercy.

But mercy is something new
in the world, isn't it? No hawk,
anyhow, ever heard of it. . . . I
even forgot, for a saving
second out there, that it ought to.

II (The Trout)

Life is simpler without it. Look,
last week a trout I had caught
flipped itself off the hook
half a second too late
and thrashed in the shallows . . . A thing
of living silver inlaid
at odd points with turquoise
and rose and topaz, little florets
on the flanks, under a mottled
olivine cape   like light
among leaves, and as lovely
(and His own *Logo* once)
as anything God ever made —
and as desperate . . . With wet hands,
I eased it back into the brook.

I still wish I knew
which of the two's worse,
when they both seem wrong —
to kill, that is, and be killed
or not quite to belong
in the universe.

Not Speaking of It

We don't speak of it. But we know.
You as well as I.
If we stop to think of it.
But why
stop to think of it? So?
We know. What is that? — The dry
wood from decades ago.
The tree grows around it. If
there's a flaw — the topsoil blown off,
the tree too tall — even so,
that slows nothing down.
It grows because it has to.

I can tell from the look in your eye
knowing was never enough.
It's wondering we live by.

"Poetry"

I admit:
I keep trying to make it, but
I don't know what it is. Would *it*
be right there in the words? Or
would the words, whether heard or seen,
be a kind of steeple, while *it* —
remote and anterior —
was a kind of sky? Something like that?

And would words, then, be disjoint
and steeples be flat —
I mean (or I think I mean)
would there be any point,
with nothing to point at?

Lines for an Order Blank

Please send seven increments of Wit
and twice that of Beauty. A bit
of Wisdom also'd be appropriate.
And another lifetime. This one
has in many respects proved inadequate,
besides shrinking since first put on
till little is left of it.

Reductio

But once out of earshot — it's odd —
out of earshot and printshot and screenshot
how implicitly one believes
every second depends now
on a permutation of cloud
or the blowdown of the leaves
or the purple of the bergamot. Not
anymore on what Men do. . . .

A saving thought . . . Although —
factor humanity out,
as five silent hills do now —
who's left, then, to tell it to?
Or to tell it? And anyhow
it's not true.

Walking Home through Woods on a Zero Night

"But nobody lives in the woods anymore."

Oh, it's true. No one belongs here.
Eastward the moon — that mad glare
of an eye with no mind
back of it, like a shark's
or a Cyclops'; and westward
the white hills it has frozen, furred
in black trees, black shadows. (Talk
about cold formality!) . . . Yet
I shouldn't have said "no mind".
Pure mind is what this is:
Moon/Earth, in their iron net
of Newtonian distances,
watching each other forever,
missing nothing — not a dead pod's
shadow on snow — and never
feeling anything. . . . Don't tell me
nobody lives in the woods,
but how one has, anywhere,
the cosmic effrontery
to face such a pair.

Versifiers

You can't call it a life. Why
do we live it?   Who even
has time to take note of us
going over our inner Niagaras
on a planking of rime — or, worse,
the odd flotsam of free verse?

Which is what we do. We can't help it
if cries are wrung from us, cries
no different in principle
from a crow's — only, because
we are word-proud and not crows, we turn
to the laws of language, the pre-
dilections of style — in part,
to be sure, for cause, but
even more for effect. . . . Things
would be different if we had wings,
even a crow's, let alone
the gyrfalcon's airfoil, if we
could ourselves be ideograms
brushed on bright air — or if
we could shake out over our heads
an arras of cascading stars
like the peacock's. . . . We can't. It's words
that deliver us. . . . Man, woman or child, we play
Pygmalions to ourselves, sculpting
in units of vibrating air, something
we pray passes for human. Here
I have hidden half a fine day
behind blinds, like an Elephant Man,
battering at English for a face.

On Looking in All Directions

*". . . a time when the universe was infinitesimally
small and infinitely dense. . ."*
       — Stephen Hawking
*". . . If we find the answer . . . we would know
the mind of God."*
      — Ibid

You've lived in the universe
(or some kind of verse)
some number of years. Been told
this and that about it. And now,
having stepped outside in the dark,
you look up at it yourself.

. . . Best done at this time of year
in the stupendous clarity
zero cold gives, as though
the dome of intervening air
were frozen into a lens
bringing everything nearer
and brighter — Lyra, Orion, Draco,
The Bear, hard to discern
in the blizzards of littler stars
now visible in and among them . . . .
And all those (so you've been told)
blowing due outward, an arc
of the Big Bang, the Great
Centrifuge, detonating
into infinity . . . Yet —
you can't help noting once more —
in such iron fixity of form
men have watched for a thousand years
the same constellations. . . .

163

                                    What
holds them? (You want to ask.)
Moreover, how did wild light,
the aboriginal Einsteinian *E*,
vaulting across Nothingness,
get locked into *M*atter at all?

So you guess at a Gravity more
like James Jeans' electron, com-
prehensible only
as ". . . *a wish or emotion*": a Gravity
that is not mindless, not mere
Force or mere Torque, but *Desire* —
like a ruined billionaire's,
to recoup a totality misered
in the black-hole of a negative
forever before Time began — and this
Desire haunting all space, its traplines
like the minefields of Sadam
laid at all points. You posit

Opposed Imperatives, one
outward, the other inward,
a Mazda and Ahriman
like half-billion-mile-an-hour
headwinds to each other,
eddying into atoms,
into the ponderable world

and the ponderable world
marbled with them: the fan
of the peacock, the Iliad
war and peace, politics, everything
to the quasars and beyond,
marbled with them; even love
marbled with them: that Past

that won't let go — its mother-
tongues, memories of place,
moral laws laid down; that Future
that won't let stop —
relentless with mornings
and constant to nothing
but its own velocity. Surely

you've known both, from inside,
like a salmon, fresh water and salt
and the rip between, where the two
tear at each other . . . . You'd

inquire of the learned astronomer
whether lungs and bladder and heart hadn't
the requisite equations: Ex-
pand/Contract . . . . You,
alone there at a point in the cosmos,
Whitman-like, looking up
"in perfect silence at the stars" — and,
in no disdain of the world,
simply, between Gravity
and Levity, pissing on it   one more
question-mark in the snow . . .

A Memorandum
to the Age of Reason

To Senator George Mitchell
of the State of Maine

attn.   Gen. George Washington, Chairman
        Mr. Wm. Jackson, Esq., Secretary
        Delegates, Deputies

Item I
in re: *receipt of original transcript dated July, 1787*

Yr. proposed Constitution
for a United States of America,
due in part to my own dereliction
and in part to known laws of chronology,
arrives on my desk two centuries
later than post-date, already
ratified, in force, and amended
twenty-six times. Though no longer
of legal relevance, some response
seems appropriate, to this lens
through which the Enlightenment — or,
as we style it, the age of reason —
transmits itself into the future;
in particular as that future,
to you an impenetrable vortex
of vapors and shadows, to us
is already time-past, a trans-
fixed and immutable tableau
(so to speak) of marbles and bronzes
without breath or motion. However,
I shall pass over these, the Dates
in Latin, the Monuments. (You will receive
under separate cover a compendium
of the History of the United States — glossary
included.) My modest hope is,
in the light of these Articles,

to present certain notes, reflections
of a private citizen in the year A.D.
nineteen hundred and eighty-eight
(well assured that one need not scruple
to impose on your time who either
have none at all or the whole of eternity).

Item II
in re: *the nature of the instrument*

Above all, what is it?
It is not literature,
though it has its rhetoric. . . . Say
a legal document. But
(or therefore) a moral one:
. . . *to form a more perfect Union* . . .
secure the Blessings of Liberty . . .
(all those inalienables of person and property
declared for at Independence). A kind
of juridical *I Ching*, then:
a book that is not a book
but a living being, or
in this case a hall full, a convention;
and to be consulted (if not
conjured with: six pages,
a hexagram of a sort!) Ah, Fathers,
do you gavel for sanity still,
or again, in a wilderness
of binary numbers and mono-
manias, a nuclear autumn
of Mutual Assured Destruction (MAD)?

Or are these the bill coming in
for the Old Wilderness, killed off
and logged off and sold off
because there was no *reason*
to doubt the illimitable bounty
of a continent, a world, a Future?
Fathers, is it too late
to broaden the scope of the inquiry? —
Toward the mouse and the atom;
toward the whales and the stars; finally
to the mind that inquires — to
its reasons, to Reason itself?

Item III
in re: *a definition*

That the word *reason* denotes:
an operation of the mind (as in law
or science) in accordance
with etiological norms
derived from the "Natural World;"
which, curiously, has produced
homo sapiens and his reason, which
now holds hostage that same
natural world and reason itself
and hence all science, all law
all history and human time
past present and future . . .

That Reason can wreck a world
but not make one, the question

remaining: can it save one? . . . We look
for a law to transcend law. We take
for a paradigm our own
spontaneous prodigy of compromise . . .
How good is it? Can it hold?
Can anything hold — let alone
against human avarice — hold
against human kindness multiplied
by a terrifying fecundity?

Item IV
in re: *Article VI (" . . . no religious test shall ever
be required as a qualification to any office . . .")*

That here the Age of Belief ends
on the point of a goose quill
and the Age of reason — secular,
continental — is open for business . . .

Gentlemen, Fathers, Founders,
a belated point: We must note
that belief in the power of Reason
as supreme and optimal arbiter
in human affairs is belief still.
It's the old curse of mathematics:
No system can prove those axioms
on which it rests as a system.
You would answer: Two hundred years
of freedom is proof enough. However
certain free men — the black
hunters of the valleys of the Niger,

the red hunters of the Alleghenies,
who did not segregate Reason
from clouds, mountains, storms,
totems, and the deeds of their fathers — you
deemed part of "mere brute creation". . . .

It is still adjudged reasonable
to have founded the federal structure
on a human atrocity — black
slavery — never once mentioned lest
half the founders walk out. But Reason
cannot include that courtesy
among the blessings of liberty. Gentlemen,
what's done is done, whether in passion,
in belief, or in reason. The point
is epistemological: Liberty?
Whose Liberty? And to do what? And Reason?
Who's to say what is reasonable
and who to deny it? The system
can't prove itself; only approve.

Item V
in re: "Natural History"

No wonder we turn sometimes
away from men altogether
beyond reach of the Voices
to that Ur-world that exists — somehow
it still exists — without questions,
simply living its laws . . . Lord,
even at a crow's cawing far off

on a winter morning, nothing
to do with us — some
errand of its own cross-
country cross-cloud cross-
wind — one can be shivered, blown away
into the irrefutable . . .

Item VI
in re: *the President, the Atty. General, the*
Brigadier (ret.), Senators, Representatives, et al.

1
That after two hundred years
what remains of the Age of Reason
is the Syllogism of Sleaze:
'I am an honorable man.
Therefore what I do to prosper
is honorable. If the law
forbids it, the law's wrong . . .'

2
That honor comes to be measured
in degrees of impunity . . .

Item VII
in re: *the preamble*

We the People of the United States
in order to form a more perfect Union,
establish Justice, insure
domestic Tranquility, provide
for the common defense, promote
the general Welfare,
and secure the Blessings of Liberty
to ourselves and our Posterity . . .
I take it
any interests not listed here
are less than vital.

Item VIII
in re: *a General Admonition*

That civilized men are nostalgic
for a freedom to be found only
in Enemy Country where no
laws apply; or in wilderness
where no laws exist; where a kind
of ecstatic terror excuses
every brutality. Thus
the more civilized the more violent.

Item IX

in re: the inconsistencies:
Union vs. Secession
Justice vs. the trail of Tears
Tranquility vs. Civil War, Panic, Depression, Riot
Defence vs. Aggression, Empire
Welfare vs. Pollution, Despoliation
Liberty vs. Slavery, Bureaucratic Paranoia

That all these antinomies,
and others, resolve at the touch
of the term "Power" (*Power:*
the capacity to preserve
or better one's lot, whether
by force or by art . . .)

That both sexes, in all times
under all systems, pursue it —
a few without scruple, the rest
for protection against the few . . .

That the rhetoric and passion
for freedom, justice, decency
propagate among the oppressed,
be the oppression real or imagined . . .

That fifty presidential and one-
hundred congressional elections,
rhetoric aside, concerned Power . . .

That here is the Historian's Stone. (Apply
ad lib. to the Public Record, or
to the heart's dark heterodoxies.)

Item X
in re : *"The Philadelphia Miracle"*

That two hundred and one years ago
our Fathers brought forth in Philadelphia,
between the collapse of the Past
and the void of the Future,
a new al-chemic of government
addressed to these questions: How
shall the best be preserved
and the worst survived? . . . that they found
the Historian's stone and applied it,
coming up with a science of man, A Manual
of Practical Comity . . .

That we see in it pride of race
and pride of conviction and pride
of power — a continent
for the taking; a war won —
but nevertheless the Law
above any man and his pride . . .

It is there yet. *"In America*
we have no common race,
no common language,
no common religion.
We have only the Law. . . ."

Thus Senator Mitchell (D., Maine)
to a public miscreant
in the year 1987.

Can the Law hold? —
When those sworn to uphold it
can "plausibly deny"
having had time to read it?
Can the Law hold
when every blood, culture and tongue

from all seven continents
clamors at it for parity?
Can the Law hold
when comity among men — even
all men — is no longer enough
and the world groans at us — seas
a sewer, the raindrops a curse? Gentlemen
of the City of Brotherly Love,
can the Law hold and not hold only
but broaden, a check and a balance
between such brothers as we are
and this nightmare trashing of the Earth?

Item XI
in re: *a January Thaw*

That water wearing at ice
wears at a form of itself, i.e.
water that's turned to stone;

as tyrant and torturer
are forms of ourselves, i.e.
human, but heart-of-stone . . .

The water is repelled, but
in the long run, as we say,
wears away any stone.

will it ever wear away
its own capacity
to turn into one?

Item XII
in re: *Realistic Assessments*

That I've aged into a face
pig-lidded, chop-fallen, a scare-
mask and *memento mori* . . . That
the U.S isn't looking good either:
hypocrite, paranoid, bully,
assassin of the so-called
free world, caught murdering
and lying one week and crying
"Credibility" the next . . . (Because
the U.S must *Grow*, understand,
having borrowed the sun and the moon;
while in fact, like myself, it is shrinking,
near the last of the capital: one
continental land-mass plus
the odd archipelago taken
by force or by fraud . . .) Is that it?
No. I must note also
that a great arc of the sky, dark blue,
and brushed with wingform ap-
ricot-colored clouds at this
very instant in the west almost
makes everything O.K. . . . Well,
not coming to the end, maybe,
of ego and Old Glory, but
having been here at all.

Item XIII
in re: *a Suggested Resolution*

'That whereas we are not one people
but a miscegenation of peoples holding
in common *Only the Law* Therefore
be it urged on the several States
that all school children, prior
to graduation and requisite thereto
have the United States Constitution's
Preamble by rote and in English.'

Item XIV
in re: *Hearing, and Hearings*

Deermice in the cabin . . .
What they don't eat they chew up
for bedding . . . GET LOST! NO MICE!
I roar at one, not five feet
from me. He never looks up.
Goes on with his zigging and zagging
from speck to speck. . . . Although
he's mostly all head and the head
mostly all ears, either
he hears nothing at these
stentorian frequencies
or nothing must interfere
with his speckulations. Well,
in a bug, you could understand it.
They're in some other dimension.

But a fellow mammal with lung
and tongue and a squeak of his own
and the Supreme Law of the Place
being thundered from on high
and him oblivious — both
to the quality and the quantity
of the announcement! It's
un-nerving. Especially
when you think of Poindexter, North,
Casey, or, bordering on
the eponymous, Meese.

Item XV
in re: *the Executive Branch*

"The word *covert*," smiles the Admiral,
"has no statutory meaning." The
committee is silent, non-plussed.
Though none seems disposed to do so,
all are left to extrapolate:
'Therefore a covert operation
cannot be defined; it lacks
all semantic friction. Therefore
certain concurrent allegations
involving narcotics, mining
of harbors, murders, mutilation,
subversion, contumacy, contempt
of World Court and the congress,
relate to a non-thing and thereby
are logically and legally

irrelevant. . . .' (My God
The blandness of it! I always
thought there'd be a great roaring
this close to a black hole!)

Item XVI
in re: *a suggested 27th Amendment*

1
Whereas the race *homo sapiens*, having
overrun and subjugated the earth,
desolating and poisoning sections thereof,
now threatens instant or gradual
destruction to the rest, Therefore

Be it resolved: That Man
may no longer number among his freedoms
that of refusing his stewardship;
that the phrase "general welfare" henceforward
be constructed as referring to the earth
and all its inhabitants, plant
and animal (excluding such
microbes, insects and parasites as
from time to time might be designated)
and to their natural habitats;
and that acts of Congress addressing
social, commercial and diplomatic
matters be framed accordingly
and their results monitored accordingly.

2.
'That the Congress be, and is, directed
to frame and pass procedural rules
as well as general laws
in furtherance of the above.'

Item XVII
in re: *a plan to suspend the Constitution*
"... in case of ... violent dissent"

It was on TV. The whole country
saw it, or could have, that brief
flutter at the Hearings — the matter
mentioned, then smothered. . . . I thought
of Jefferson's ". . . firebell in the night. . . ."

Here was more than the bell: the fire
itself — muffled out on the podium
with exemplary dispatch, yes;
but the blur and the sting of it over
everybody in America since
like a weather-inversion. Fathers,
I had not thought, even at worst,
we had come to this. Abe Lincoln,
as sworn, stood to the text
through five years of civil war. Who
are these men who can't hold it
against a parade of placards? Fathers,
as you live in it, this charter
should have dripped blood and tears
down the wall where those legacides,

to-a-man sworn to protect it,
covertly then — and covertly still,
undeterred by the chance exposure —
plot to suspend it. *Suspend it!*
On what authority? What man
or what men, in what numbers
or in what combination of powers
granted under it? On whom
will a grateful nation heap honors
for propping it up again
like death-in-life, like a scarecrow,
a Halloween effigy, once
this thing's done: the great words,
the great breath "suspended"? Fathers,
let us call a garotte a garotte
and the curse of the world on it.

Item XVIII
in re: *Second and Third Thoughts*

What the hell's the difference (they say);
you can't change things; your Public's
a Great Beast; let each
look to his own soul . . . .

May be

said souls have a tax to pay
for leaving whatever star
they flew from to this fix
where soul downshifts into flesh-
and-blood and the unalterable
into politics.